Milan

Trieste
Venice

A
P
E
N
Genoa
N
Florence
Pisa
I
N
E
S

Corsica

ROME

Sassari

Naples

Sardinia

T y r r h e n i a n

S e a

Cagliari

I o n i a
S e a

Palermo

S i c i l y

Syracuse

A d r i a t i c   S e a

M E D I T E R R A N E A N

S E A

The ITALIAN WAY

Aspects of Behavior,

Attitudes, and Customs

of the Italians

MARIO COSTANTINO
LAWRENCE GAMBELLA

New York Chicago San Francisco Lisbon London Madrid Mexico City
Milan New Delhi San Juan Seoul Singapore Sydney Toronto

The *McGraw·Hill* Companies

Library of Congress Cataloging-in-Publication Data

Costantino, Mario.
    The Italian way : aspects of behavior, attitudes, and customs of the Italians / Mario
Costantino, Lawrence Gambella.
      X, 120 p.: map ; 23 cm.
      Includes bibliographical references (p. 117) and index.
      ISBN 0-8442-8072-0
      1. Italy—Social life and customs—1945–

DG451 .C67   1996
945—dc21   96-22120

10 11 12 13 14 15 16 17 18 19 20 21 22 23 24 VRS/VRS 0 9 8 7

ISBN-13: 978-0-8442-8072-1
ISBN-10:   0-8442-8072-0

McGraw-Hill books are available at special quantity discounts to use as premiums and
sales promotions, or for use in corporate training programs. For more information, please
write to the Director of Special Sales, Professional Publishing, McGraw-Hill, Two Penn
Plaza, New York, NY 10121-2298. Or contact your local bookstore.

This book is printed on acid-free paper.

CONTENTS

CONTENTS

INTRODUCTION

This prefatory note is meant to briefly introduce our study of Italy on the threshold of the twenty-first century. The reader must not be under the misconception that a great nation such as Italy, so rich in history and culture, can be comprehensively described in any single volume. Rather we are dealing here in broad strokes. The variety of topics encompassed herein presents general aspects of Italian life as witnessed today. We have focused on presenting snapshots of daily life, which the reader can easily comprehend and identify with. So you will find articles about food, gestures, celebrations, and customs. Our descriptions are meant to stimulate curiosity and pique one's interest for more in-depth research into Italy—a nation moving head-long into the future while keeping its traditions of yesteryear. A visit to Italy is always an exhilarating and educational experience—and we hope that you will experience a bit about life in Italy vicariously through these pages.

NOTE ON ITALIAN PRONUNCIATION

Italian is easy to pronounce. Many vowels and consonants are pronounced as they are written, without the variation of sound-symbol correspondence found in English. The following chart gives guidelines for pronouncing Italian words. It will help you pronounce the words you see in this book. Note that the syllables in capital letters are stressed.

Vowels

Italian Letter	Sound	Examples
a	ah (yacht)	caro [kAH-roh], dear
e	eh (bet)	piede [pee-EH-deh], foot
e	ay (bay)	perché [pehr-kAY], why/because
i	ee (fleet)	bambini [bahm-bEE-nee], children
o	oh (scope)	nazione [nah-tzee-OH-nay], nation
o	o (north)	nonna [nOHn-nah], grandmother
u	oo (fool)	luna [lOO-nah], moon

Consonants

Italian Letters	Sound	Examples
ci	chee (cheese)	cibo [chEE-boh], food
ce	chay (chafe)	cena [chAY-nah], supper
ca	kah (comic)	capo [kAH-poh], head, chief
co	koh (cone)	colore [koh-lOH-reh], color
che	kay (cake)	perché [pehr-kAY], why, because
chi	kee (key)	banchi [bAHn-kee], desks
gi	jee (jeer)	gita [jEE-tah], trip
ge	jay (June)	generalmente [jay-nay-rahl-mEHn-teh], generally
gh	gh (spaghetti)	traghetto [trah-ghAYt-toh], ferry
gli	ly (familiar)	figli [fEE-ly-ee], children
gn	ny (companion)	compagno [kohm-pAH-ny-oh], friend
qu	kwah (quack)	quaderno [kwah-dAYr-noh], notebook
sce	shay (shaker)	pesce [pAY-shay], fish
sci	shee (she)	scimunito [shee-moo-nEE-toh], crazy
z or zz	ts (beats) or dz (beads)	piazza [pee-AH-tsah], square
		zero [dzEH-row], zero

1. APRIL FOOLS' DAY

The first day of April has long been called April Fools' Day from the custom of tricking people on that day. The Italian equivalent of April Fools' Day is called **il pesce d'aprile.** People play tricks and pranks on friends and associates, who may be sent on foolish errands. They realize that they are being taken for a ride when they hear someone shout **Pesce d'aprile!** (April fish).

No one knows for sure the origin of the custom of playing tricks, and you will find many theories put forward. In April, religious representation in the Middle Ages depicted scenes from the life of Jesus, who was sent back and forth from Pilate to Herod and from Herod to Pilate. This may have given rise to the custom of sending people on fruitless errands. Others trace the origin of the day to France where, sometime during the sixteenth century, the great writer and humanist, François Rabelais, played a prank on the royal family. Rabelais wrapped up some brick dust and labeled it ''poison.'' For this, he was brought to Paris as a traitor. When his jest was discovered, people started calling the fooled party ''un poisson d'avril'' (un pesce d'aprile). Whether this is because fish tend to be easily caught in April or because the sun was leaving the zodiacal sign of Pisces (the fish) during this season, no one knows.

2. AT THE TABLE

A tavola non s'invecchia (People do not get old at the table). Food and drinks are part of the "brio" of life. Mealtime is always a happy and very sociable time! The family gets together to enjoy the food, discuss family matters, talk about daily events, or just gossip.

Manners are extremely important: so sit up straight, no elbows on the table, napkin on your lap, and wait for everyone to be served before starting to eat. Use your silverware correctly in the European way. Cut your food with your knife in your right hand and bring the food to your mouth with your fork in your left hand. Do not switch your fork from left to right after having cut the food. Bring the food to your mouth with the tines of the fork down. To indicate that you have finished eating, place your fork and knife or spoon parallel to each other across your plate. To indicate a pause in eating, place them facing each other.

Pasta in every form and shape is almost always on the menu. It is always a separate course and not served with the meat course. Meals may have several courses, including **antipasti**, salad, cheese, and nuts. A large meal often ends up with a "shot" of **sambuca** (licorice-tasting liqueur) or **amaretto** (almond liqueur) and is topped off with an **espresso** (strong black coffee). (See article 38, "Meals and mealtimes.")

At a restaurant, waiters are to be shown respect and treated with courtesy. They are food connoisseurs and many of them are linguists capable of conversing in several languages. They may recommend house specialties and suggest the best drinks. Water and condiments are not automatically placed on the table. You may have to ask for **un'acqua minerale** (mineral water) and wait for a waiter to season your food or ask for salt (**sale,** sAH-lay) and pepper (**pepe**, pAY-pay).

3. ATTRACTING ATTENTION

Pardon! or **Scusi!** for "Excuse me!" and **Per favore** or **Per cortesia** for "Please" can be used to attract someone's attention. They are used in speaking to people who are relatively close by.

For a person some distance away, you would use **Ascolti!** or **Senta!** You might use **Ascoltate!** and **Sentite!** or **Ascoltino!** and **Sentano!** These are the command forms of the verbs *ascoltare* and *sentire* (to hear and to listen). When they are used to attract attention, they more or less convey the idea of "Hey there!"

Here is a summary of use:

Attention-Getting Word	Pronunciation	Use
Scusi Ascolti Senta	skOO-see ah-skOHl-tee SEHn-tah	Used with an unfamiliar adult or casual acquaintance **Scusi, cameriere!** (Hey there, waiter!)
Scusate Ascoltate	skoo-sAH-teh ah-skohl-tAH-teh	Used when you address a group of people or can be used with an unfamiliar or older adult
Ascoltino Sentano	ah-skOHl-tee-noh sEHn-tah-noh	Used when you are addressing a group of people **Ascoltino! È loro questo?** (Hey there! Is this yours?)

Attention-Getting Word	Pronunciation	Use
Ascolta Senti Ma senti! Che fai?	ah-skOHl-tah sEHn-tee mah-sEHn-tee kay-fAH-ee	Used to attract the attention of a friend, a family member, or a child. They are informal singular *(tu)* command forms of *ascoltare* and *sentire*. They are also used to convey annoyance in speaking to adults with whom you would normally use the formal **Ascolti!** and **Senta!**

Signore! (sir!), **Signora!** (ma'am!), and **Signorina!** (miss!) may also be used to attract the attention of someone either close by or far away. If your intention is to ask for information or a favor, you should introduce the request with some polite word or phrase.

Signore becomes **Signor** when it is followed by the name of the person's occupation.

Signor vigile! (Officer!)

Signor dottore! (Doctor!)

In bars and very informal restaurants, such as sidewalk cafes, the waiter may be called in ways that are not commonly used in English-speaking cultures, such as snapping the fingers or saying *psss!* once or twice.

4. "BAD LUCK" DAY

In our culture, Friday the thirteenth is considered to be a day of bad luck. The Italian equivalents are Tuesday and Friday the seventeenth. The days of martedì (Tuesday) and venerdì (Friday) are considered unlucky days, probably because they are derived from the names of Mars, the Roman god of war, and Venus, the Roman goddess of love. Both gods caused trouble for mortals. There are even sayings that reflect this belief:

Di Venere e di Marte né si sposa né si parte.

(On Friday and on Tuesday, neither marry nor embark.)

The number seventeen is viewed in card and number games as **la disgrazia,** bad luck—especially in southern Italy. Strangely enough, the number 13 is worn around the neck as a good luck charm. (See article 36, "*Il malocchio*" for more information on Italian superstitions.)

5. *IL BAR*

Il bar *(café)* serves many functions in the daily life of Italians. It opens early and closes late. It is an attractive and familiar establishment where local people and passersby mingle to enjoy the coffees, pastries, and sandwiches capable of pleasing even the most discriminating palate.

In the morning, the bartender prepares **espresso** (strong coffee) and **cappuccino** (coffee with steamed milk), and serves pastries such as **cornetti** (croissants). Customers eat a quick breakfast while standing at the counter. On the way to work, school, or office, people hustle and bustle into the neighborhood bar.

At noon, people rush in and grab a **panino** (sandwich) and a drink.

During the day and at night, the bar is a gathering place for people to share **un gelato** (ice cream) and drinks with friends. There, the arguments of the day—ranging from politics to sports or personal matters—are discussed, analyzed, and critiqued over a card game or the reading of newspapers. The bartender is a familiar figure who always seems to know everyone and everyone's affairs.

The bar always occupies a central location on the main avenues, in the piazzas, and on street corners. The flashing neon lights and the outdoor display of chairs and tables with umbrellas (when the weather is nice) signal its location. The bar may be the last stop to share a soft drink, a pastry, or **un caffè** (a coffee) with the family after the evening **passeggiata** (stroll).

There are several customs with which tourists should be familiar. In many bars, customers need to pay and get a receipt (**uno scontrino**) before ordering at the counter. In addition, it often costs considerably more to sit down and have something to drink or eat than it is to have the same item standing up at the bar.

6. *LE BARZELLETTE*

The Italian dictionary defines **la barzelletta** as a "witty little story." This definition cannot in any way convey the rich meaning and importance of *la barzelleta* in Italian culture. Jokes and sayings change over time, and one could say that *barzellette* reflect the tastes and preferences of different periods. But it is also true that in spite of changing styles, situations, and characters, laughter is generated by the same feelings: embarrassment, irony, and the desire to laugh. Every place (at a bar with friends, strolling, at the dinner table, at work, or at school) and every situation gives the Italians a pretext to *raccontare una barzelletta* (tell a joke).

Telling a joke is an art and the best joke tellers become very popular among friends. *Barzellette* for Italians are safety valves that allow them the opportunity to poke fun at everything and to relax and release tension through laughter.

There are books on *le barzellette*. They include the best of the Italian jokes and help the reader get a good laugh and escape the monotony of daily life. (See the "Related Readings" section at the end of this book.)

7. BASIC EXPRESSIONS IN ITALIAN

The following expressions are basic to polite conversation in Italian. People in Italy are generally friendly and very receptive. A person in uniform, a waiter, a store clerk, or anyone else may be approached when you need to ask for information. Smile, be very courteous, and use the one of the following appropriate expressions to express your wants and needs.

Mi scusi.	mee skOO-see	(Excuse me.)
Per piacere.	pEHr pee-ah-chAY-reh	(Please.)
Per favore.	pEHr fah-vOH-reh	(Please.)
Buongiorno.	boo-OHn jee-OHr-noh	(Good morning.)
Buona sera.	boo-OH-nah sAY-rah	(Good evening.)
Un momento.	OOn moh-mEHn-toh	(Just a second.)
Va bene.	vah bEH-nEH	(That's OK.)
(Mille) grazie.	(mEEl-leh) grAH-tsee-eh	(Thank you.)
Prego.	pREH-goh	(You're welcome.)
Sì.	see	(Yes.)
No.	noh	(No.)
Signore	see-ny-OH-reh	(sir)
Signora	see-ny-OH-rah	(madam)
Signorina	see-ny-oh-rEE-nah	(miss)
Potrebbe dirmi . . .?	poh-trAYb-beh dEEr-me	(Could you tell me . . .?)

Potrebbe aiutarmi?	poh-trAYb-beh ah-ee-oo-tAHr-mee	(Could you help me?)
Come sta?	kOH-meh stAH	(How are you?)
Dio ti benedica!	dEE-oh tee beh-neh-dEE-kah	(May God bless you!)
Mi dispiace.	mee dee-spee-AH-cheh	(I am sorry.)
Grazie, non c'è di che!	grAH-tsee-eh nohn cheh dee kAY	(Don't mention it!)

8. *LA BEFANA*

In Italian tradition, **la Befana** is a fantastical being in the shape of an old woman who brings children gifts on the eve of Epiphany (January 6). She walks on the rooftops carrying a bag filled with toys and treats for the good children and ashes and charcoal for the bad ones. She comes down the chimneys and leaves gifts in the stockings, open shoes, and sandals left out by the children.

Today, Italian families, while respecting the tradition of *la Befana,* have also accepted **Babbo Natale** (Father Christmas or Santa Claus), who brings gifts on Christmas Eve. It is not unusual to see La Befana and Santa Claus parading together in the streets of Italian cities and to see Santa Claus greeting children and speaking to them in stores. However, be careful. Using the expression **Che befana!** to a woman is making fun of her appearance.

9. BUSINESS

Italy ranks among the major industrialized nations of the world, along with the United States, Japan, Germany, Canada, France, and England. This is true despite the fact that the country's territory is less than one half of the size of the state of Texas, and its mineral resources are few. While northern Italy is one of the most advanced industrial areas of Western Europe, southern Italy, because of its rocky terrain, is poorer and less progressive. (See article 64, "The two faces of Italy.") Nonetheless, Italians, with their creativity, dedication, and hard work, are skilled competitors in the modern business world.

The success of many businesses sits on a solid foundation: the family. In family businesses, most of the members are involved in the organization and running of daily operations. Many of Italy's largest companies are family-run, such as Fiat by the Agnelli family.

Personal attention plays a very important role in daily business transactions. The customers deal directly with business owners and are treated with courtesy and respect—even in the bargaining process, which is an expected part of doing business.

Numerous small entrepreneurs keep alive Italy's centuries-old tradition of quality. Many artisans are engaged in the production of local arts and crafts, which are popular at home and abroad. When visiting Italy, tourists should become acquainted with the variety of products that regions, cities, and villages have to offer. (See article 56, "Shopping.")

Large chain stores can be seen throughout the peninsula, but businesses carrying family names are still a clear indication that the family-oriented business, with its application of skill and taste to production according to aesthetic principles, is still the backbone of the Italian industrial success.

There is another side to the business situation in Italy. In recent studies, Italy has risen in the ranking of industrialized nations when the black market is taken into account. Some experts estimate that the black market accounts for 20 to 30 percent of Italy's gross national product. The black market is work done outside of normal channels, and it is not taxed. The nontaxed industries involved in the black market include the making of purses, shoes, and fake designer jeans. Those engaged in these cottage industries may see them as a way to make extra money or a way to stay off the dole.

Business hours

Opening and closing hours are very flexible in Italy and vary from place to place and according to the season. Don't be surprised to see signs in businesses such as **Chiuso oggi** (closed today) and **Chiuso questo pomeriggio** (closed this afternoon).

Many retail stores close during the mid-afternoon, between 1 and 4 P.M. However, they may be open until 7 or 8 in the evening. Restaurants are usually closed between 3 and 6 P.M. Offices and chain stores may close for a few hours in the early afternoon between 1 and 4 P.M. and stay open until early evening. Most banks are open from 8:30 to 1:30, and some may open again for one hour, from 3 to 4. Post offices are open six days a week, from 8:30 to 2 P.M. Monday through Friday and until noon on Saturday.

Pharmacies in an area are open on a rotation basis on holidays and Sundays. The local newspapers give names, addresses, and telephone numbers of **le farmacie di turno.** Smaller stores close for vacation periods during the summer.

As a tourist, you will notice that museums vary in their opening and closing hours, and it is best to check in advance to find out when they are open. Most of them, however, are closed on Mondays. Many churches close in the early afternoon and open again about 4 P.M.

10. *CALCIO* (Soccer)

Forza, Italia! Forza, azzurri! are the cheers chanted by Italian fans to urge on their national soccer team during international competitions. The Italian national team traditionally is a strong one and it has won the World Cup Soccer championship three times, second only to Brazil, which has four to its credit, and equal to Germany, which also has won three. Names of players such as Meazza, Piola,

Colaussi, and Paolo Rossi (affectionately called "Pablito") will always be remembered by Italians as great champions who led their teams to World Cup victories. Here is a summary of the results of Italy's World Cup victories, useful background information to have before you attempt to discuss sports with Italians:

1934	Italy 2, Czechoslovakia 1	(in Rome)
1938	Italy 4, Hungary 2	(in Paris)
1982	Italy 3, West Germany 1	(in Madrid)

Although Italy lost in the finals to Brazil in 1994 in Los Angeles, the star of the team, Roberto Baggio, was awarded **il pallone d'oro** (the golden soccer ball) for that year for being the best soccer player in the world.

Soccer traces its origins in Italy to the Renaissance. In Florence, the game was elegant and picturesque. Teams were composed of twenty-seven players, who were allowed to use both hands and feet when playing ball. The large square in front of the church of Santa Croce served as a soccer field. During the same period, Venetians played soccer on a round field, and the goal line was marked by cement steps.

When did the modern game of soccer start in Italy? The date given is 1887, when English people residing in Italy introduced the sport to the country. In 1893, the "Genoa Cricket and Foot-ball Club" was founded, the oldest Italian soccer association. The **Federazione italiana del foot-ball** (Italian Soccer Federation) was organized in Turin on March 15, 1898. During this period, the first Italian soccer championship took place. It was played in one day among only four teams. Genoa, the **Internazionale** of Turin, the **Foot-ball club torinese,** and the **Ginnastica** of Turin. (The Genoa team won the championship, by the way). On March 15, 1910, in the Arena of Milan, the Italian national team played in its first international competition. Italy won the match against the French team by a score of 6 to 2. Gradually soccer competitions were organized throughout the peninsula. Almost every town had its own **squadra di calcio** (soccer team).

The period between 1934 and 1940 is viewed as the "golden years" of Italian soccer. During the period, Italy won the World Cup twice (1934 and 1938), an Olympic title (1936), and in thirty-six consecutive matches gained twenty-four victories, six draws, and no defeats! Despite recent successes, the national team has experienced no greater period.

Today organized soccer within Italy encompasses many levels. At the top are the eighteen best teams in the country that participate in the **campionato** (championship) and belong to **la serie A** (The "A" group); at the bottom is **il calcetto** of local neighborhood competitions. On Sunday afternoons, stadiums are packed as fans come to see the top league games. People are interested in their **squadra del cuore** (favorite team). It is an explosion of enthusiasm. The various teams compete in popularity and ignite rivalry in the same town. Before and after the games, fans gather at bars, in the open-air piazzas, and at the workplace to "comment" on the games. Everyone has a version of the events. If the game is lost, **il portiere fa le papere** (the goalkeeper ducked the ball), **hanno sbagliato tattica** (their tactics were wrong), **l'arbitro è cornuto** (the referee is a fool), **il centravanti s'è mangiato il gol** (the forward missed). When the game is won, **la squadra è in forma** (the team is in top form), **il giocatore ha fiuto e sfonda sempre** (the player has a very good nose and always knocks the bottom out of the net), **il centrocampista è una colonna, un asso** (the center forward is a pillar, an ace), **il portiere è un gatto e vola fra i pali** (the goalkeeper has the agility of a cat and can fly from pole to pole), **il numero dieci è un genio** (number 10 is a genius). Other expressions you might hear as soccer is discussed are these: **Che mazzata!** (What a hit!), **Che parata!** (What a block!), **Che contropiede!** (What a counterattack!) or **Ma non è farina del suo sacco!** (I think someone else had a finger in the pie!) The opinions are varied and abundant. The soccer tournament is a gigantic kaleidoscope through which the fans can see what they want to see. Radio and television broadcasters pitch in with their comments to extend the dispute before and after the next soccer match. It is the other championship of the network (radio vs. television): Rai vs. Finivest. The roster for the Rai group is **Novantesimo Minuto** and **Domenica sportiva** (RaiUno); **Domenica Sprint**, and **Dribbling** (RaiDue); **Processo del lunedì** and **Scusate l'anticipo** (RaiTre). The lineup for the Finivest (the television group) is on Italia Uno, **L'appello** del martedì and **Domenica stadio; Pressing, Studio sabata,** and **Guida al campionato**.

In Italy, the soccer players receive the highest salaries in the world and only the best "stranieri" (foreigners) are recruited to play in the country. Today, Italian soccer is tormented by political, technical, and financial crises. The overdose of soccer on television has reduced the number of fans at the stadiums. The prices of tickets are too high and people tend to shy away. Perhaps the key men, Gianluca Vialli, Giuseppe Giannini, Dino Baggio, Giovanni Bia, Giuseppe Signori, and Franco Baresi will have enough energy and talent to attract larger groups of fans to the game.

Fans, fanaticism, and violence

Soccer has become a **sport di massa** (a sport that attracts large crowds of people). When fans gather at stadiums, there can be—and has been—violence. From one viewpoint, soccer should help fans let out their frustrations by a discharge of energy in cheers and jeers. Yet in the past, at major soccer events, violence has erupted and people have been killed or injured, sometimes when one group of fans attacks another. In the mid-1990s, the Italian soccer league stopped play in the middle of the season as protest against the violence.

There has traditionally been rivalry among teams. Particularly strong are the rivalries between teams from the same area (for example, between Milan and Inter, between Torino and Juventus, between Genoa and Sampadoria, and between Roma and Lazio). It is a ritual for opposing factions to antagonize one another with insulting banners such as *Devi morire* (You must die). The traditional rivalries may be carried on in equally insulting songs.

An organized fanatic display of support for teams has developed, and it has created a new culture that includes slogans and songs and organized cheers with the props of banners, streamers, musical instruments (drums, trumpets, and horns), and firecrackers. The city of Verona is the motherland of **gli ultras** (superfans), and there the well-known sport magazine **Supertifo** is published. In the "soccer" dictionary, the words **riti** (rituals) and **gemellaggio** (friendly relationships) have taken on a new meaning. *Riti* are the soccer slogans and cheers. *Gemellaggio* means that the *ultras* of two different teams decide to support one another. For example, there is *gemellaggio* between the teams of Verona and Inter, Milan and Bologna.

Singing is an important part of soccer rituals. In Milan, the fans of the Milan team (which is called the **rossoneri** from its vertically striped red and black jersey) sing the following:

Rossoneri siamo noi,
Ma chi . . . siete voi?
Noi del Milan siamo qua
E per voi non c'è pietà.

We are the red and black fans
Who are you?
We, the fans of Milan, are here,
And we will not have any mercy on you.

The soccer fans borrow both new and old themes for their songs. The most popular tune has been *Guantanamera*. Fans have also adapted the music from the Triumphal March from Verdi's *Aida*, and *Eine Kleine Nachtmusik* by Mozart.

For more information on Italians and sports, see article 58, *"Lo sport."*

11. CALENDAR

The first day of the Italian work week is **lunedì** (Monday), and **sabato** (Saturday) is a workday for many. **La settimana lunga** (the long week) has six workdays, while **la settimana corta** (the short week) contains only five.

In the English-speaking world, weeks are considered to consist of seven days; in Italy, weeks include both the beginning and ending days. As a result, what we refer to as a week is referred to as a period of eight days, and a two-week period as fifteen days.

Partiamo fra otto giorni.	(We are leaving in a week [eight days].)
Partiamo fra quindici giorni.	(We are leaving in two weeks [fifteen days].)
Partiamo oggi a otto.	(We are leaving a week from today [from today in eight days].)
Partiamo oggi a quindici.	(We are leaving two weeks from today [from today in fifteen days].)
Passammo otto giorni là.	(We spent a week [eight days] there.)
Passammo quindici giorni là.	(We spent two weeks [fifteen days] there.)

In Italian, the full date is written in a different order from what we may be accustomed to: first the number of the day, then the month, then the year. The measures of time go from the smallest (the day), to the next size (the month), to the largest (the year).

20 **maggio** 1995	(May 20, 1995)
3 **febbraio** 1996	(February 3, 1996)

When numbers are used to stand for months, they follow the same pattern:

20–5–1995	(5/20/95)
3–2–96	(3/2/96)

The expression **fare il ponte** (to make the bridge) indicates a holiday period of three or more days when a workday is sandwiched between two holidays. For example, if Assumption Day falls on a Tuesday, Monday would be an additional day off for many workers (since Sunday is also a holiday). Monday is the bridge between Sunday and the holiday. The extended vacation may also be referred to as **il ponte:**

Per il Ponte di Capodanno andremo in Montagna.	(We will go the mountans for New Year's vacation.)

12. CALLING CARDS

Calling cards, **biglietti da visita,** are commonly used in Italy in social situations and in business. They typically give information on a person's level of education and job and are an indication of a person's social status. The quality of the paper selected for the card and its design show the person's taste. The cards can be used as a vehicle to introduce oneself on any occasion. College graduates use them to show off their newly received degree, which entitles them to the title of **dottore.** They may, however, cross out their title with a friendly smile before handing out their card. Simple calling cards have a person's name, degree, address, and telephone number. The more sophisticated ones have a person's name, title, residence, business address, home phone, business phone, telex, and fax numbers.

13. *IL CAMPANILISMO*

Campanilismo is described as a strong attachment to one's village or birthplace. It refers to local sentiment, and it is especially felt in the **Mezzogiorno** (the area south of Rome) and in Sicily. The word derives from **campanile,** the village bell tower. The bell tower dominates the **piazza,** which is the heart of the village and the center of all activities. The term *campanilismo* implies trust and love for the people within the same community, living within the sound of the bell tower—one's **paesani** (fellow townspeople), who constitute a kind of extended family. Given the mountainous terrain of Italy, villages perched on the hills and mountainsides found communication with the outside world difficult until the advent of railroads, cars, radio, television, and telephones. People could only count on other local townspeople for help and survival.

14. *IL CARNEVALE*

Carnevale or **Carnovale** is a period of fun, noise, and confusion. According to different traditions, it starts on January 17 or February 2 and culminates in dances and masked balls. In any case, it is a period of celebration before the Christian season of Lent, the period of fasting before Easter. People play pranks on one another because **Di carnevale ogni scherzo vale** (During carnival time, anything goes). Celebrations vary from town to town with masquerades that reenact local traditions and historical events. Firecrackers, **il palo della cuccagna** (climbing the greasy pole), horse races, and the competitions among neighborhoods add color to the festivities.

On the last day, people parade in the streets and throw streamers while following elaborate floats. Some parades may end with the burning of a mannequin called *Carnevale* to symbolize the end of the days of abundance and the beginning of Lent. In Italy, the most famous carnival is **Il Carnevale di Viareggio.** (Viareggio is a resort on the Tuscan coast.) The carnival in Venice is also well known and features historical costumes.

15. CELEBRATIONS AND HOLIDAYS

Festa is a word that has magic. It may mean a party, a holiday, or a festival. *È festa* when family and friends get together. *È festa* if people do not have to report to work. *È festa* when the feast of the patron saint or a historical event is celebrated with a street festival. Street decorations, bands, displays of fireworks, religious processions, and sport competitions such as climbing a greasy pole may be part of the celebration!

The term **festa nazionale** refers to an official national holiday. Many religious holidays are official holidays, even though the celebrations have religious origins, such as Assumption Day. This is a sign of the importance of religious traditions in Italy. National government offices, including the post office, are closed, and private businesses may be shut down. The official national holidays are supplemented by many local or regional holidays that may last one or more days.

Festa is part of many expressions. The expression **È finita la festa!** (The party's over!) is an idiomatic sentence that means "We have fooled around up to now. Let's get serious!" But while **fare la festa a una torta** means "to enjoy eating one's cake," **fare la festa a qualcuno** (to give someone a party) means abusing or even killing a person.

Religious celebrations

These are the main religious celebrations in the Italian world:

Epifania   Epiphany, January 6
La Befana, the fantastical being in the shape of an old woman, carries a bag filled with gifts. On the night of January 5, she leaves toys for good children and coal and ashes for bad ones. (See article 8, **La Befana.**)

Mercoledì delle Ceneri   Ash Wednesday
Ashes are distributed and the season of Lent begins.

Domenica delle Palme   Palm Sunday
Branches of olive trees are blessed and handed out to the faithful.

People exchange the palm as a sign of peace. In many villages, farmers plant a branch in the fields in hope of a bountiful harvest. (This may be as a remembrance of a pagan ritual paying tribute to spring.)

| **Giovedì Santo** | Holy Thursday |
| **Venerdì Santo** | Good Friday |

Worshipers visit churches that have displays of the Santo Sepolcro (Holy Sepulchre).

Pasqua   Easter Sunday

Church bells toll joyously. People have already mailed Easter cards to friends and family members, and now they greet each other with **"Buona Pasqua"** (Happy Easter). At dinner, the children read letters, previously prepared in school, to their parents. In these, the children promise to be good and as well behaved as their parents would like them to be. Their immediate reward is an embrace, a kiss, and a few **lire** (some spending money). **La colomba pasquale** (Easter cake in the shape of a dove) and **l'uovo di Pasqua** (the chocolate Easter egg), elegantly adorned in colorful paper wrappings and containing a gift of some sort, are given as presents.

Lunedì di Pasqua   Easter Monday

Spring is here and everyone is eager to go for **una scampagnata** (a trip to the country). Rustic food, music, and dancing welcome the arrival of spring. This is a time for short vacations and school trips.

Ascensione   Ascension Thursday (forty days after Easter)

This religious holiday commemorates Christ's Ascension into heaven. In some areas of southern Italy, shepherds give free milk to neighbors. People may eat macaroni with milk and wash their faces with rose petals.

Corpus Domini   Corpus Christi (Body of Christ)

Corpus Christi is a popular holiday throughout Italy. It is marked by religious ceremonies and the pageantry of processions with people in historical costumes. Many towns decorate their streets with flowers arranged in biblical scenes. These may cover the pavement for hundreds of yards. While the religious processions wind down the road, people throw rose petals from their balconies and open windows.

Assunta   Assumption, August 15
Special foods are prepared after mass to commemorate the Blessed Mother's assumption into heaven. It is the **Ferragosto** (vacation) period in Italy. Tourists crowd the Italian cities while Italians escape to holiday resorts. (See article 23, *"Il Ferragosto."*)

Tutti i Santi   All Saints' Day, November 1
Tutti i Morti   All Souls' Day, November 2
People remember their dead family members and friends. They visit cemeteries, bring chrysanthemums, and light candles.

Immacolata Concezione   Immaculate Conception (December 8)

Natale   Christmas, December 25
Presepi (Nativity scenes) adorn homes and churches. Shepherds travel from town to town filling the air with the sound of Christmas carols played on their bagpipes. People buy **il panettone** (cake with raisins) to be given as a present to family and friends.

Public holidays

Here are the main public holidays. Many are the same as the religious ones.

Capodanno   New Year's Day
Il Veglione di Capodanno (New Year's Eve party) is a festival of food, music, and dance to welcome the new year. Towns set off displays of fireworks. At the stroke of midnight, Neapolitans open the windows and throw out old dishes and furniture.

Epifania   Epiphany, January 6

Festa della Liberazione   Liberation Day, April 25
This commemorates the liberation of Italy from the Germans at the end of World War II, in 1945.

Lunedì di Pasqua   Easter Monday

Festa del Lavoro   Labor Day, May 1

Ascenzione   Ascension

Corpus Domini   Corpus Christi

Festa della Repubblica   Proclamation of the Republic, June 2 (celebrated on following Saturday). It is celebrated by military parades and musical performances.

Ferragosto   Feast of the Assumption, August 15

Tutti i Santi   All Saints' Day, November 1

Immacolata Concezione   Immaculate Conception, December 8

Natale   Christmas holidays, December 25 and 26 (**Santo Stefano**)

Local celebrations

Almost every town has its special celebrations that trace their roots far back into the past. These folkloric events are survivals of the religious and secular traditions that regulated the life of the peninsula throughout the centuries. Competitions, regattas, jousts, and processions often have as a stage and background a piazza, palace, or monument. These festivals are unforgettable experiences in which people relive the customs of the past.

February

Il Festival della Canzone Italiana   San Remo (Italian Riviera, Liguria) (Italian Popular Song Festival)
This is a competition to select the best song. Foreign singers can

participate as guests and sing in their native language, but they cannot compete.

Carnevale   Viareggio (Lucca, Tuscany)
This features a splendid parade of colorful and allegorical floats.

Il Festival di Bacco   Verona
(Bacchus Festival)
Bacchus, the mythological god of wine, brings back memories of the past in a celebration of harvest.

March

La Festa di San Giuseppe   March 19
(Saint Joseph's Day)
Many places have **la festa del giglio** (feast of the lily, a symbol of Saint Joseph). In Naples, in Calabria, and in other regions of southern Italy, people make **ciambelle** (ring-shaped cakes) and **frittelle** (sweet fried dough).

Festa della Primavera   Rome
(Spring Festival)
This is a local folk festival with typical Roman cuisine, songs, and dances.

April

Domenica delle Palme   Taranto
(Holy Week Festival)
Palme (palms) are branches of olive trees. The processions in Taranto are well known throughout Italy for their Spanish roots and rituals. People in masks and white robes with pointed hoods parade through the streets.

Adorazione della Croce   Rome, Florence, Good Friday
(Adoration of the Cross)
In Rome, the pope performs the Stations of the Cross from the Colosseum to the Palatine Hill.

Pasqua   Rome, Florence
The many Easter ceremonies in Rome culminate in the papal blessing "Urbi et orbi" (To the City and the World). In Florence, there is the **Scoppio del carro** (explosion of a cart). The explosion is sparked by a dove that slides on a suspended wire from the high altar in the cathedral to fireworks outside.

May

Maggio Musicale   Florence
(May Music Festival)
This is a famous music festival that includes Renaissance music and costumes.

Festa di Sant'Elisio   Cagliari, May 1
(Feast of Saint Elisio)
This includes processions to honor Sardinia's patron saint.

Festa di San Nicola   Bari, May 8
(Feast of Saint Nicholas)
This is a procession of fishing boats.

Sagra del Pesce   Camogli (Liguria), second Sunday in May
(Fish Feast)
People fry fish in a giant pan.

Corsa dei Ceri   Gubbio (Umbria), May 15
(Race with Candles)
This is one of Italy's most noted processions. In it, tall shrines are carried to a church at the top of a mountain.

Palio del Balestrieri   Gubbio (Umbria), last Sunday in May
(The Palio of the Archers)
This consists of a crossbow contest.

Cavalcata Sarda   Sassari (Sardinia), Ascension
(Mounted Procession)
This is Sardinia's most popular folk festival with a costumed procession in the morning and traditional songs and dances in the evening.

23

Infiorata   Genzano (Lazio), Corpus Christi
(Flower Festival)
The town has elaborate flower displays.

Raduno del Costume e del Carretto Siciliano   Taormina, end
of May
(Festival of Costumes and Sicilian Carts)
Festival of traditional costumes with the traditional hand-painted
Sicilian carts illustrating the stories of Knights of the Round Table,
the Paladins of Charlemagne, and **i Pupi,** the classic Sicilian puppets.

June

Gioco del Ponte   Pisa, first Sunday in June
(Bridge Festival)
This is a race with historical boats.

Festival dei Due Mondi   Spoleto (Umbria), mid-June to mid-
July
(Festival of Two Worlds)
This is an international festival of music, dancing, and drama. It
also features film screenings, modern art shows, and displays of local
crafts.

Gioco del Calcio   Florence
(Historical Ball Game)
It is a contest of strength and skills between competing neighbor-
hoods. There is also a procession in sixteenth-century costume.

July

Il Palio   Siena, July 2 and August 16
Arguably, this is the most famous and hotly contested of all traditional
games. It consists of a horse race that takes place in the main piazza
of the city, pitting one neighborhood against another for the *Palio*,
a banner. (See article 44, *"Il Palio."*)

Festa di Santa Rosalia   Palermo, July 10–15
(Feast of Saint Rosalie)
This celebration honors the patron saint of Palermo.

Festa de' Noantri   Rome, July 15
This is a ten-day celebration held in the Trastevere neighborhood of old Rome. Folk dancing and singing and mass spaghetti eating occur simultaneously.

Stagione Lirica   Verona, July and August
(Opera Season)
Operatic festival featuring elaborate productions is held in the **Arena di Verona,** an ancient Roman amphitheater.

August

Mostra d'Arte Cinematografica   Venice, August and September
(Film Festival)
This international festival awards prizes that are among the most prestigious in the world of cinema.

Torneo della Quintana   Ascoli Piceno (Marche), first Sunday in August
(Joust of the Quintana)
This historical pageant features jousting.

Festa dei Candelieri   Sassari (Sardinia), August 14
(Procession of Candles)
People in Spanish dress carry huge wooden candles.

La Sagra degli Gnocchi   Opi (Abruzzo), August 24
This feast features **gnocchi** (a kind of dumpling).

Settimane Musicali   Stresa (Piedmont), August 25 to September 20
(Music Festival)

September

Giostra del Saracino   Arezzo (Tuscany), first Sunday in September
This is a historical joust.

La Regatta   Venice
This is the famous historical regatta on the Grand Canal.

Festa di Piedigrotta   Naples, September 6 and 7
This is a folk song festival.

Luminara di Santa Croce   Lucca (Tuscany), September 13
(Feast of Lights)
This features religious processions.

Dante Celebrations   Ravenna, mid-September

Levante Fair   Bari
This display of goods from all over the world lasts for ten days.

Festa di San Gennaro   Naples, September 19
(Feast of Saint Janarius)
People wait in nervous expectation for **il miracolo,** the liquefaction of Saint Janarius's blood. Saint Janarius is the patron saint of Naples.

October

Festa di San Francesco   Assisi, October 4
(Feast of Saint Francis)
The feast of the patron saint of Italy is marked by religious ceremonies and singing throughout the town, which is illuminated at night.

December

Presepi   mid-December to mid-January
There are nativity scenes in churches throughout Italy, some of which are very elaborate with many detailed figures.

✸

16. COMPLIMENTS, APPRECIATION, AND CRITICISM

Italians are warm and charming people. The manner in which their ideas are expressed in words indicates their feelings and character. The expression of the voice, or a look or intonation, manifest personal reactions toward persons and situations. The Italian language, so rich and so colorful, compliments, enhances, and embellishes each word and expression with its harmonious sounds. Nonetheless, it is important to be familiar with people and surroundings when interacting either to compliment, to criticize, or to gossip. Regions, cities, and villages may have different historical, social, and economic backgrounds. People may be sensitive to unsolicited remarks or compliments coming from strangers or mere acquaintances. Generally speaking, it is always nice to be diplomatic and Italians are diplomats.

Compliments

Admiration

Che bella ragazza!	kay bEHl-lah rah-gAHt-zah	(What a nice girl!)
Che carina!	kay kah-rEE-nah	(How nice!)
Che simpatica!	kay seem-pAh-tee-kah	(How nice!)
Signora, quel vestito le dona molto!	see-ny-OH-rah, koo-AYl veh-stEE-toh leh dOH-nah mOHl-toh	(Madam, that suit flatters you!)
Che elegante!	kay eh-leh-gAHn-teh	(How elegant!)
Ma che tipo!	mah kay tEE-poh	(What a guy! What a girl!)

27

Che figo!	kay fEE-goh!	(What a hunk!)
Che fusto!	kay fOOs-toh	(What a hunk!)
Grazie. Lei è molto gentile!	grAHt-zee-eh. lEH-ee EH mOHl-toh jehn-tEE-leh	(Thank you. That's very nice!)

Praise

Complimenti!	kohm-plee-mEHn-tee	(Congratulations!)
Hai fatto una figurona!	AH-ee fAHt-toh OO-nah fee-goo-rOH-nah	(What an impression you've made!)
Ma che bravo!	mah kay brAH-voh	(How great!)
Ma quanto è gentile!	mah koo-AHn-toh eh jehn-tEE-leh	(How considerate you are!)
È in gamba!	eh een gAHm-bah	(You are great!)
È un fenomeno!	eh oon feh-nOH-meh-noh	(You're phenomenal!)
È proprio un cannone!	eh prOH-pree-oh oon kahn-nOH-neh	(What a dynamo!)
Grazie del complimento.	grAHt-zee-eh dAYl kohm-plee-mEHn-toh	(Thank you for your compliment.)

Regard

Scusi!	skOO-see	(Excuse me!)
I miei rispetti!	ee mee-EH-ee rees-pEHt-tee	(My respects!)
Mi compiaccio con lei.	mee kohm-pee-AH-chee-oh kohn lEH-ee	(I congratulate you.)
Mi dispiace.	mee dee-spee-AH-cheh	(I am sorry.)
Grazie, non c'è di che!	grAHt-zee-eh. nohn ch-EH dee kay	(Thanks. You're welcome!)

Respect

Buon giorno, dottoressa!	boo-ohn jee-OHr-noh, doht-toh-rAYs-sah	(Good morning, doctor!)
Buona sera, signore (a)!	boo-OH-nah sEH-rah, see-ny-OH-reh (ah)	(Good evening, sir!)
Professore! Come stà?	proh-fehs-sOH-reh kOH-meh stAH	(How are you, professor?)
Dio ti benedica!	dEE-oh tee beh-neh-dEE-kah	(May God bless you!)

Criticism

Fa schifo!	fa skEE-foh	(Disgusting!)
Guarda che pasticcio hai combinato: complimenti!	goo-AHr-dah kay pahs-tEE-chee-oh AH-ee kohm-bee-nAH-toh: kohm-plee-mEHn-tee	(What a mess you have made: congratulations!)
Non vale niente!	nohn vAH-leh nee-EHn-teh	(It's not worth it!)
Non sa fare niente.	nohn sah fAH-reh nee-EHn-tee	(He/she doesn't know how to do anything.)
Si crede di essere non so chi.	see crAY-deh dee EHs-seh-reh nohn soh kee	(He/she really thinks that he/she is something.)
Si da' tante arie.	see dah tAHn-teh AH-ree-eh	(He/she's stuck up.)
È tutto fumo e niente arrosto.	eh toot-oh fOO-moh ay nee-EHn-teh ahr-rOHs-toh	(It's all smoke and no fire.)
Fa la civetta.	fah lah chee-vAYt-tah	(He/she's a flirt.)
Che buffone!	kay boof-fOH-neh	(What a clown!)

17. DATING AND MARRIAGE

Italy is a modern country where new and old ways of life coexist and complement each other. Today's young generation lives in a world dominated by all the modern means of communication. Young people are better educated, more exposed to the news transmitted almost instantaneously by cable or satellite, and more aware of the new ideas affecting the behavior of youth throughout the world. Young people find it easier to express their feelings, discuss their ideas, and compare them to the rest of the world.

Portable telephones are very popular among young adults, and communication can take place almost anywhere. Young adults in Italy also have the freedom of mobility. Their cars and mopeds allow them to zoom through the neighborhoods and from city to city. Beach, mountains, and local resort areas, along with schools and workplaces, are ideal points of encounter for members of both sexes. Larger cities in Italy are cosmopolitan centers where interaction with people from various countries is part of daily life.

Young adults in Italy feel free to date and marry as they wish. **Il ragazzo** (boyfriend) or **la ragazza** (girlfriend) may be introduced to the family. When things become serious the couple **si fidanza** (becomes engaged) and, in some regions, the families get together to celebrate the event with **un bel pranzo** (a fine dinner). The **anelli di fidanzamento** (engagement rings) may be exchanged and plans for the wedding are made. The old traditions surface, and respect for the family must be shown. When the young couple have jobs, the wedding expenses are paid by them. If help is needed, **la dote** (the dowry) is still the responsibility of the bride's family, while the groom's parents may provide the house or apartment.

The wedding date is announced through elaborate **partecipazioni** (wedding invitations). The bride dresses in white and the groom in formal attire. They are accompanied by **le damigelle** (bridesmaids) and **i cavalieri** (ushers). The **papà** gives away the bride at the foot of the altar. Certain churches and shrines are traditional sites for weddings and are still chosen by young couples. The church ceremony is both a civil and religious event and is followed by a reception or a dinner.

The nuptial reception is usually elaborate. Many delicious dishes satisfy the palate of the most demanding guest and there is lively music. Even though weddings vary from town to town according to local traditions, every couple begins married life with **la luna di miele** (the honeymoon). The couple thus becomes part of the extended family and gains its place among friends and relatives.

18. DRIVING IN ITALY

Cars, mopeds, and motorcycles are the mainstay of transportation in Italy.

Mopeds, vespas, and scooters are fast and economical. They give people—especially young people—mobility, a chance to show their driving ability, and comfortable seats when they chat with friends in a **piazza** (square), at the corner, or in the park. The roar of the motorcycle signals one's presence—and this roar is commonly heard on Italian streets.

Most cars are small or mid-size. They can be parked easily and consume less gas, which is very expensive in Italy.

Driving in Italy can be hazardous. Towns and villages may have narrow winding roads with no traffic lights at intersections. Large round mirrors on buildings and walls help drivers see the vehicles coming from the opposite direction or from hidden corners. Further complicating driving may be a series of one-way streets, which make it difficult to get from one place to another without knowing the street system. On mountain roads, people may honk to signal their presence as they wind their cars around blind curves.

Today Italy's picturesque byways have been superseded by a well-developed system of superhighways called **autostrade.** For the most part, they are less scenic but faster, smoother, and more modern. The autostrade by virtue of their nature have cut across sections of the countryside and rural communities and connected them to the outside world, making even the most outlying town accessible in a fraction of the time it took thirty years ago.

In cities, there may not be traffic lights at every intersection, and trolleys and buses may be in one's way. During **le ore di punta** (rush hours), there may be long lines of traffic (**le code**), and arguments may ignite at intersections as some drivers try to get ahead. **Il vigile** (traffic officer) may direct traffic, standing on a platform in the middle of the intersection. People who violate traffic rules may be fined and asked to **conciliare** (pay the fine) on the spot.

Highway traffic moves very fast. **La polizia stradale** (highway troopers) patrol the highways. Drivers are expected to have **la patente** (driver's license), either national or international, **il libretto** (registration), and **il bollo** (inspection sticker). A **triangolo** (a triangular sign) is carried to signal an emergency.

Tourists wishing to travel by car in Italy should get an International Driver's License, obtainable from the Automobile Association of America (AAA). If you arrive in Italy without having an international license, you may apply to the Automobile Club d'Italia. Since Italy conforms to the Geneva Convention of the Highway Code, road signs follow international standards. Speed limits are generally 50 kilometers (31 miles) per hour in populated areas, 90 kilometers (56 miles) per hour or higher on the outer main roads of towns and cities, and 130 kilometers (74 miles) per hour on the **autostrade.** The Italian government has set up twenty-four-hour emergency telephone numbers for tourists and foreigners: 116 for motorists experiencing car trouble and 06–4212 for travel assistance and directions. One should always opt for the extended automobile insurance plans when renting a car, since any mishap will be fully provided for, from injury and accidents to minor dents.

❈

19. EDUCATION

Education is compulsory in Italy for children from 6 to 14. About 90 percent of the student population attends public schools and about 10 percent attend private and parochial schools. At the age of 3 or 4, many Italian children are sent to nursery schools (**asili** and **giardini d'infanzia**). At the age of 6, they begin **la scuola elementare** (a five-year elementary school program, which is followed by **la scuola media unica** (three years of junior high). After **la scuola media**, they may choose to continue their education for five years in a **liceo** or in an **istituto**, which may be compared with senior high school and junior college in the United States. (Those who do not plan to attend a university usually go to a vocational school for three years.) The **liceo classico** offers a classical education, and the **liceo scientifico** offers scientific courses. An **istituto** follows curricula that prepare students for specialized careers in technical, commercial, industrial, agricultural, and other such fields. An **istituto magistrale** graduates elementary school teachers. Italian universities award **diploma di laurea** and the title of doctor; for example, **Dottore in Lettere e Filosofia** (doctor of literature and philosophy), **Dottore in Economia e Commercio** (doctor of economics and business), **Dottore in Medicina e Chirurgia** (doctor of medicine and surgery). The **laurea** is the equivalent of a master's degree in the United States.

Public education in Italy is free, but students have to purchase their own textbooks. One of the greatest differences between schools in Italy and those in the United States is that students must attend six days a week. The hours are typically from 8 A.M. to 1:30 P.M., but elementary schools now have **tempo pieno** (full time), when classes meet from 8:30 A.M. to 4:30 P.M., five days a week. Under Italian law it is mandatory to make religious education available, but it is not mandatory for schoolchildren to attend religious education classes, since anyone can choose an exemption. Students who attend parochial schools must pass state examinations in order to be granted a diploma.

Italian students must be prepared to pass written and oral proficiency examinations. The Italian students seldom work while attending school; learning is considered to be their primary occupation. Italian students try to make the most of their monetary allowances. They "chip in" with one another when planning trips or parties or even buying newspapers. **I quadri** (the final class marks), which are posted by junior and senior high schools in July, indicate those who have reached **la maturità** (scholastic maturity).

Being a student may mean assuming responsibility in a very competitive world. Jobs are scarce and require very high skills. When a **concorso** (an examination for a job) is announced, there may be few openings and thousands of applicants. Many are qualified but only a few will pass the stringent examination. In addition, **la raccomandazione** (one's connections) may come into play (see article 52). But many have hopes of attaining their dream jobs.

❁

20. EXPRESSIONS SUCH AS *DIO MIO!*

Saints, angels, God, Jesus, and Mary are frequently invoked by Italians in their everyday speech. Such expressions are not signs of disrespect, but are part of common speech patterns. They are generally used to add emphasis to what one is saying.

Expressions invoking God and the saints will vary from region to region. While a Neapolitan will say **San Gennaro, pensaci tu!** (Saint Janarius, take care of us!), a Sicilian may repeat **Gesù, Giuseppe, e Maria!** (Jesus, Joseph, and Mary) or **Bedda Madre!** (Blessed Mother!).

Dio sia ringraziato or **Grazie a Dio** (Thanks be to God) and **Dio sia lodato** (God be praised) are used to express gratitude and thankfulness.

In nome di Dio (in God's name) or **Per l'amor di Dio** (for the love of God) gives more force to a prayer or a request.

Se Dio vuole! Dio volesse! A Dio piacendo! Faccia Dio! Come Dio vuole! (God willing! As God wills!) express hope or resignation.

Dio ti assista (May God assist you), **Dio sia con te** (May God be with you), **Dio ti guardi** (May God keep you) are expressions of goodwill.

Dio ce la mandi buona, Dio ce ne guardi, Dio non voglia (God forbid) may even exorcize evil spirits.

O Dio! (O God) and **Dio mio!** (My God) are common forms of invocation.

To express impatience, surprise, disappointment, anger, happiness, and other strong emotions, you will hear the following: **Dio, che confusione!** (Oh God, what confusion!); **Dio buono!** (Good God!); **per Dio!** (For God's sake!); **Dio santo!** (For God's sake!); **santo Iddio!** (Holy God!); **Dio, che gioia!** (God, what joy!); **Dio, che pena!** (God, what a pain!); **Gesù, come ti trovo cambiata!** (Jesus, how it's changed!); **Gesù, che spavento!** (Jesus, what a scare!). **Non c'è Cristo, non ci sono cristi** indicates that there isn't any possibility to achieve a certain goal.

Body language, voice intonation, and pitch variations accompany the use of these expressions to heighten their communicative effect.

❈

21. EYE CONTACT IN CONVERSATION

Italians are very expressive, and, of course, the eyes are an important means of communication because **gli occhi sono le finestre dell' anima** (the eyes are the windows to the soul).

Many common Italian expressions contain the word **occhio** (eye):

A quattr'occhi indicates a face-to-face conversation.

Mettere gli occhi addosso means to show particular interest in a person.

Fare gli occhi dolci is to demonstrate a yearning or special liking for a person.

35

A mother who speaks very fondly of her children will say they are **la pupilla degli occhi,** which is equivalent to ''apple of her eye.''

Avere gli occhi foderati di prosciutto (to have one's eyes filled with ham) means not to see obvious things.

When somebody does something questionable and expects the other person to look the other way, the expression used is **chiudere un occhio** (to close an eye).

22. FAMILY AND FRIENDS

La famiglia è sacra (Family is sacred). This sentence reflects the deep feelings of love and loyalty that connect family members in Italy. The family nucleus of **papà, mamma, e figli** (papa, mama, and children) is surrounded by the extended family that includes **nonni** and **nonne** (grandfathers and grandmothers), **zii** and **zie** (uncles and aunts) and **cugini** (cousins) and also **compari e comari** (godfathers and godmothers). In small towns and villages, since many people are distantly related, the people who have even some degree of kinship are still greeted with the titles of **zio** and **zia**, such as **zia Rosa e zio Peppino** (Aunt Rose and Uncle Joe).

The oldest son usually inherits the family house, which is passed down from generation to generation. It is here where **fratelli** and **sorelle** (brothers and sisters) and their children convene to show their respect for the family patriarch. He is still consulted on family matters and blesses weddings, communions, and any other important endeavors.

Family ties are very strong. **La famiglia** (family) gets together to share joy and pain. It is a tower of strength for its members who may mourn the loss of a relative or join to celebrate a wedding of one of its members. The family is a support system that extends beyond the original place of birth. Family members living outside the family nucleus are visited when other members travel, relocate to another city, study at a faraway college, go for medical treatment, or any other occasion because **per la famiglia si fa tutto** (you do anything for the family). **Essere di buona famiglia** (to be part of a good family) is of the utmost importance for cultural, social, practical, and economic reasons. **Dimmi come via, con chi vai e ti dirò chi sei** (tell me how you dress, with whom you associate, and I'll tell you who you are) still echoes in the mind of the Italian household.

The **compare** and **comare** (godfather and godmother) are held in high esteem for religious and social reasons. They are accepted into the family and respected because they have acted as sponsors in the baptism or confirmation of a child. **Compare e comare di fede** are witnesses at a wedding (**la fede** is the wedding ring). This is another form of alliance between individuals and families.

Amico and **amica** (friend) usually refer to close friendships; **il conoscente** or **la conoscente** are simple acquaintances. **L'amico** is always ready to offer you an espresso coffee or beat you to the ticket window to pay for a movie. **Il miglior amico** and **la migliore amica** (best friend) are always treated with respect by the members of the family. The expressions **È il mio ragazzo** and **È la mia ragazza** are used when talking about a close relationship between young people who are dating without any serious commitment. They become **fidanzati** (engaged) when an engagement ring is exchanged and wedding plans are outlined. **Il compagno di classe** and **la compagna di classe** are classmates. Friendship is still deeply revered inside and outside the family. It is important **poter contare sulla famiglia e su una buona amicizia** (to be able to count on the family and on a good friend).

To the Italian, a friend is family. In some respects, a friend may be more trusted and respected since the friend is carefully chosen, unlike the family member, who is related by birth. Friendships are lasting and quite often carry on into old age. It is only when one does some **disgrazia** (harm) to another that a friendship is severed. The "forgive and forget" code is applied in many cases; however, it is juxtaposed with the principle that one may forgive, but never forgets.

Two of the most precious treasures an Italian possesses are his or her family and friends. The Italian measures wealth not in possessions but in the strong family ties and the number of friends one has. Even when a male suitor is brought into the family, the phrase that is spoken after he leaves is **Basta che è rispettoso!** (The main thing is that he respects the family). Woe be to the young man who forgets to speak respectfully and to know his place, for the man who respects not the family and his elders will prove not to respect his own wife and family later on. This is **fare male figura** (showing oneself to be ill-bred).

Those who sought **il gran destino** in the past and left Italy to go to the United States, Canada, or Australia could be excused because they needed to make a living or find a better life. Yet many of these travelers found themselves either taking trips back to the family and homeland or returning to Italy to retire to the slower pace and marvelous sunshine.

The Italians who remain in the **città** (town) and **paesetto** (village) close to the family maintain close ties by visiting several times a week or making daily telephone calls to various family members, especially parents.

23. *IL FERRAGOSTO*

August is the time of the year when Italians take vacation seriously. It is understood by all that stores, boutiques, museums, and even churches may have staggered opening hours during **Ferragosto,** August vacation time. Some businesses, in fact, open only in the mornings, closing for the day at noon. Many do not open at all. The vacation period coincides with the religious feast of the Assumption of Mary on August 15.

Ferragosto is further marked by a mass exodus of Italians from the cities by car—both to other locations in Italy and abroad. There are often reports of huge traffic jams on roads leading out of major cities. Because of Italy's proximity to other European nations, Italians think nothing of taking automobile excursions with the entire family to France, Germany, Spain, Greece, Switzerland, Austria, Holland, Belgium, and the United Kingdom. All of Europe is accessible, and gasoline prices in other countries are generally below what Italians pay in Italy—therefore, the exodus.

During this period, the major Italian cities are far from deserted. They are filled with tourists and students of culture and art from all over the world. The streets and museums are usually packed with first-time visitors as well as seasoned tourists returning for their second, third, or even fourth visit to this nation of diverse culture and spectacular art.

24. FORM OF GOVERNMENT AND POLITICS

Italy is a democratic republic. It has a parliamentary government with a president, a cabinet headed by **il presidente del consiglio** (prime minister), and a parliament consisting of **Senato** (Senate) and **Camera dei Deputati** (Chamber of Deputies).

Both houses of parliament elect the president to a seven-year term. The president is the commander-in-chief of the armed forces, can declare war, and has the power to dissolve the parliament and call new elections. The president appoints the prime minister, who forms a government. There is no vice-president. The president of the Senate serves in place of the president in case of illness. New elections are held when the president dies.

The Italian prime minister is selected from the Chamber of Deputies by the president, must be approved by the parliament, determines national policies, and is a powerful figure in the Italian political world.

Typically the prime minister is selected from one of the parties that forms the coalition that has won the most deputies in the last election. The prime minister selects the members of the cabinet, who must be approved by both the president and the parliament. The prime minister and the cabinet are referred to as **il governo** (the government). The parliament can replace the prime minister, who has no fixed term of office.

The Senate and Chamber of Deputies have equal power in passing laws. Deputies and senators serve five-year terms. There are 320 members of the Senate, of whom 315 are elected and 5 are appointed for life by the president. There are 630 members of the Chamber of Deputies.

Electoral changes are taking place in Italy. On April 18 and 19, 1993, Italians voted to change the proportional representation system of choosing members of the Senate. On June 30, 1993, the Chamber of Deputies adopted similar reforms. On August 4, 1993, the electoral reforms were written into law by parliament.

Previously, the percentage of the seats held in parliament by each party was the same as the percentage of the total votes received by the candidates of each party. There were a large number of small parties in parliament and no party had a majority in either house. The prime minister was compelled to form a government of coalitions (alliances) among parties.

The new electoral system is changed from the former proportional system. Now three fourths of the deputies and senators are elected from districts that elect a single candidate. The candidates have to campaign for individual seats. The remaining one fourth of the seats are still determined by proportional representation of the parties on the national scale. However, to obtain seats, a party must receive at least 4 percent of the vote.

There had been many political parties in the past, and governments often changed as the result of shifting coalitions between and within parties, although many of the same politicians participated in governments in different roles over the years. Italians hoped that the "Second" Republic of the middle 1990s would offer the possibility of a government that can take effective action. Other proposals are now in the air, including the possibility of a federation on the Swiss model.

Local governments derive their power from the national government. Italy is divided into twenty regions. The regions consist of provinces, and every province is made up of many communes. Each province and each commune has an elected **consiglio** (a one-chamber council) and a **giunta** (an executive body). The province is governed by an elected council and by a prefect appointed by the Minister of the Interior. The commune has a mayor who is elected directly by the people.

The Italian Judicial System. All judges, except fifteen of the Constitutional Court, are appointed, not elected. Five are selected by the president, five by the Parliament, and another five by other courts. The other judges earn their appointments by passing civil service examinations. The Superior Council of Judiciary is composed of a panel of twenty-four judges. They and the National Ministry of Justice regulate all court operations. The highest court in Italy is La Corte Costituzionale, the Constitutional Court. There are several lower courts: the Court of Appeals (appeals from civil and criminal courts), the Court of Assizes (serious crimes), and the Courts of Cassation (reviews decisions of lower courts and returns cases to them for new trials).

The legal code of Italy is based upon the Napoleonic Code of Justice. Under this code, a person is guilty until proven innocent. A defendant must provide his or her own defense in the form of **un avvocato** (an attorney) or represent himself or herself.

25. GALLANTRY

Italians manifest their feelings very openly. They have a special taste for a beautiful, intelligent, and attractive person. In Italy, men truly appreciate a woman who is attractive, nicely dressed, seductive, and charming. Men whistle and say things when they want to compliment her. They may say **Che bambola!** (What a doll!); **Che bella ragazza!** (What a lovely girl!); or **Signora, quell'abito le dona molto!** (Madam, that suit enhances your beauty!). Italian men have a gleam in their eyes and a smile when they bow to formally greet a lady with **il baciamano** (kissing of the hand). Such open manifestations might surprise others from less demonstrative cultures. When a girl or woman flirts playfully with men, the expression heard is: **Che civetta!** (What a coquette!). **Che befana!** (What a witch!) is shouted or whispered after a woman who may not be attractive. The verbal display of gallantry may be accompanied by the famous **pizzico** (pinch) or **la mano morta** (the touching hand).

Women express their admiration for a man by saying **Che fusto!** (What a hunk!) or **Vieni qua cocco di mamma!** (Come here, darling!). When they are annoyed by unwanted advances they may say: **Cretino! Imbecille! Smettila!** (Stop it, stupid!) or **Che cafone!** (What a jerk!).

26. GESTURES

Gesturing is an essential element of communication in Italy. Body talk is as natural as speech. It adds emphasis and color to one's personal expression. Anger, happiness, and almost any other feeling can be expressed without saying a word. This "silent language" may differ from town to town and reflect local cultural traditions. Neapolitans are masters in the art of gesturing.

27. HOUSES AND HOUSING

When we think of going home in the United States, we may envision a house with two floors, with five or six rooms on the first floor and three to five rooms on the second floor. We would add to that a garden or lawn surrounding the house, with a backyard and a patio. In contrast, homes in Italy in many towns are up to three stories high and attached to the surrounding houses. Their balconies may overlook medieval streets and be draped in overhanging flowers. **Le tendine** (curtains) provide some shade during siesta time. **Le persiane** (heavy shutters) keep the cold out in winter and keep the coolness in during the summer.

An alternative to the house would be modern condominium apartments (**condominio**), that are common in cities. Condos can have spacious rooms and high ceilings; others are designed to make the best use of a smaller space. The space available is supplemented by a balcony, where people may eat in nice weather.

Villas are being constructed today on mountainsides and seashores, and some are within the financial reach of a working person. On the other hand, crowded high-rise complexes housing many families in a small space may be found on the outskirts of major cities. As with its geography, there is great diversity in Italian housing.

28. INTRODUCTIONS

To the Italian, respect is cardinal, and therefore one is expected to demonstrate a sense of propriety when meeting someone for the first time. One's upbringing is judged by the manner in which a person conducts himself or herself at this first meeting. First impressions are lasting impressions and will weigh heavily in the family's acceptance of a new friend.

When being introduced to one another, two men will extend their hands and firmly, but not aggressively, grip the other's hand while saying **Piacere** (a pleasure). When a man is introduced to a woman, he should not extend his hand to her unless she extends hers first.

After people are well-acquainted or when a relative is being greeted, a person may extend the right hand and kiss both cheeks of the other person—yes, even when two men greet one another. Affection is an integral part of respect, and therefore everyone engages in a kissing ceremony at the beginning and the end of a visit, a street encounter, or after mass on Sunday morning.

Informal introductions among young people and adults are quite simple. Here is an example.

ANTONIO:	Ciao, Anna. Questa è la mia amica Maria.	Hello, Anna. This is my friend Maria.
ANNA:	Ciao! Piacere.	Hello. It's nice to meet you.
MARIA:	Ciao, come stai?	Hello, how are you?

In formal presentations, a man is introduced to a woman and the younger person to the older. The presenter always asks for permission before any introduction.

LUIGI:	Scusi, professore! Posso presentarle il mio amico?	Excuse me, Professor. Can I present my friend?
PROFESSOR:	Certamente!	Of course!
GIANCARLO:	Buongiorno, professore, Sono Giancarlo Marchese.	Good morning, Professor. I'm Giancarlo Marchese.

❁

29. ITALIAN FILMS

The Italian film industry has had a long history. In the early part of the 1900s, the industry was noted for many historic epics, often based on Roman history. The studios at *Cinecittà* (Cinema City) in Rome became the center of the film industry after World War I. However, to many people, the great age of Italian film was the period after World War II, when the realistic style of Italian films influenced the style of films worldwide.

Roberto Rossellini, Federico Fellini, Luchino Visconti, Michelangelo Antonioni, Carlo Ponti, Lina Wertmuller, and Nanni Moretti are among the best-known and most respected Italian filmmakers.

Roberto Rossellini (1906–1977) is considered the father of neorealism, the style that characterized Italian films after World War II. Neorealism featured social realism, popular settings, and political commitment. Rossellini's classic works are *Roma, città aperta* (*Rome, Open City,* 1945), which is set in wartime Rome and stars Anna Magnani; *Paisà* (1946), another film set during the war; and *Stromboli, terra di Dio* (1951), set on the island off Sicily. Later in his career, Rossellini directed many historical and biographical films: *La presa del potere di Luigi XIV* (*Louis XIV's Taking of Power,* 1966), *Atti degli apostoli* (*Acts of the Apostles,* 1968), *Pascal* (1971), and *L'età di Cosimo* (*The Age of Cosimo de'Medici,* 1973).

Federico Fellini (1920–1993) moved from reality to surrealism and metaphor in his career, which included films such as *I vitelloni* (1953), *La strada* (1954), *La dolce vita* (1960), *Satyricon* (1969), and *Amarcord* (1973). Fellini's *Otto e mezzo* (*8½,* 1963) is a semiautobiographical work that tells the story and fantasies of a beleaguered film maker.

Luchino Visconti (1906–1976) also started in neorealism. He later focused on the lifestyle of the aristocracy to show individuals' anxiety, frustration, and isolation. His films include *Ossessione* (*Obsession,* 1942), based on the book *The Postman Always Rings Twice; La terra trema* (1948), about the life of a poor Sicilian fishing community; *Il Gattopardo* (*The Leopard,* 1963), on aristocrats at the time of the unification of Italy based on the novel by Tomasi di Lampedusa; *La caduta degli dei* (*The Damned,* 1969); and *Morte a Venezia* (*Death in Venice,* 1970).

Michelangelo Antonioni (1912–) also started in neorealism but developed an abstract personal style that made him one of the most controversial film makers of the sixties. His films include *L'avventura* (1959), *La notte* (1960), *Blow-Up* (1966), and *Zabriskie Point* (1969).

Lina Wertmuller (1928-) uses comedy to treat many serious issues—politics, feminism, consumerism. She delights in using dichotomies—the south versus the north, poverty versus affluence, progressivism versus conservatism, industrial versus rural. Her films include *Mimí metallurgico* (*The Seduction of Mimi*, 1971); *Travolti da un insolito destino nell'azzurro mare d'agosto* (*Swept Away*, 1974); *Settebellezze* (*Seven Beauties*, 1976); and *Ciao, Professore* (1994).

Nanni Moretti (1953-) analyzes contemporary Italian society in comedic fashion. One of the more distinctive characteristics of Italian life may be viewed in *Caro Diario* (*Dear Diary*, 1994), which is a mixture of comedy and stoic political satire. *Palombella Rossa* (1989) is a thoughtful critique of the Italian Communist Party, told by a water polo player.

Equally famous are a number of Italian performers, including Sophia Loren, Gina Lollabrigida, Marcello Mastroianni, Giancarlo Giannini, Totò, Vittorio Gassman, Nino Manfredi, Monica Vitti, Laura Antonelli, Franco Franco, Ciccio Ingrassia, Giuliano Gemma, Mario Merola, Ugo Tognazzi, Alberto Sordi, and Vittorio De Sica. They epitomize the Italians in all circumstances and predicaments because they live and breathe the Italian experience of **La vita! Che vita! La mia vita! L'Italiano!** (Life! What a life! My life! The Italian!).

❇

30. ITALY ON WHEELS

The best way to see Italy is by car. You have the opportunity to go where you want and stay where you want. Most of all, you have the chance to explore picturesque Italy, weaving through pastoral mountainsides or along coastal roads and stopping where you want to sample the local dishes or visit the local sites. This article presents you with an imaginary itinerary, pointing out major things to see. (Note, however, that cars are often a detriment in major cities, where traffic is heavy and frantic and parking places impossible to find. See also article 18, "Driving in Italy," and article 63, "Transportation."

Suppose you plan to rent a car in Rome and travel northward to Florence. Stop at Perugia, which is 117 miles from Rome and is one of several of Italy's picturesque historic towns that have kept a great deal of their medieval character. Here are sites to see in Perugia:

- La Fontana Maggiore: A large fountain dating from the thirteenth and fourteenth centuries featuring sculptures by Nicola and Giovanni Pisano.

- Palazzo dei Priori: A government building in the Gothic style begun in the thirteenth century with a magnificent staircase. This is on the same piazza as the fountain, the Piazza 4 Novembre, which is the heart of the old town.

As you walk the streets of the city, you may hear many languages other than Italian being spoken. This is because Perugia is the home of a well-known university for the teaching of Italian to foreigners.

Then take a side trip to Assisi (16 miles east of Perugia), which is well worth the detour. This is the city where the medieval saint Francis lived and worked. This picturesque city on a hillside contains many magnificent medieval churches, which include:

- Basilica di San Francesco: It contains the tomb of Saint Francis, who founded the Franciscan religious order of mendicant monks in 1210. It also has precious frescoes from the thirteenth and fourteenth centuries. The fresco cycle in the upper part of the church depicting the life of Saint Francis is attributed to Giotto.

- Santa Chiara: This church, on a terrace overlooking the countryside, has the tomb of Saint Clare, a contemporary of Saint Francis, who founded an order of nuns.

If you happen to visit Assisi on October 4, which is the feast of Saint Francis—who is the patron of Italy—you will encounter street festivals throughout the town, with performers singing traditional songs and doing traditional dances from one of the regions of Italy.

Now you're on your way north to Florence. But, again, a stop along the way at Siena, a city with a medieval character, is advised. These are the must-see places.

- Piazza del Campo: One of the most famous squares in the world, shaped like a scallop, with eleven streets leading into it. There the *Palio* is run (see article 44).

- Palazzo Pubblico: The medieval town hall of Siena contains major works of art by the Sienese artists Ambrogio Lorenzetti (an allegory of good and bad government), Simone Martini, and Taddeo di Bartolo.

- Duomo: The town's cathedral is recognizable by its horizontal bands of green and white marble.

- Pinacoteca: This museum is a veritable treasure house of Sienese painting of the Middle Ages, noted for its decorative fantasy and graceful line.

If art galleries, cultural events, and shopping are high on your agenda, plan a long stay in Florence, or as the Italians call it, **Firenze** (172 miles north of Rome). Florence is home to many of the splendors of Renaissance art, including painting, sculpture, and architecture. Here are just a few of the sites:

- Santa Maria del Fiore: This is the cathedral, or **Duomo,** of the city. It was begun in 1296 by the architect Arnolfo di Cambio and its magnificent dome is by the Renaissance architect Brunelleschi (1434). If you walk to the top, 348 feet high, you will have a magnificent view of the town.

- Battistero di San Giovanni: The baptistery standing nearby the cathedral is decorated in patterns of white and green marble, which is characteristic of many Florentine Romanesque churches. One of its bronze doors was called by Michelangelo the doors of Paradise. They depict Biblical scenes and were designed by Ghiberti in the early fifteenth century.

- Galleria degli Uffizi: This museum contains a dazzling collection of Renaissance painting including Botticelli's *Primavera (Springtime)* and *Nascita di Venere (Birth of Venus),* famous Annunciations by Simone Martini and Leonardo da Vinci, as well as works by Giotto, Piero della Francesca and Masaccio, to name just a few. The museum is in a Renaissance palace, which served as government offices under the Medici rulers of Florence.

- Palazzo Pitti: In another Medici palace, this museum houses a remarkable collection of paintings, including works by Raphael.

- Accademia: This museum contains works by Michelangelo, including his *David*.

- Cappelle Medici: The works in these Medici chapels include Michelangelo's tombs for Giuliano de' Medici and Lorenzo II de' Medici.

- Santa Croce: This church of the Franciscans has tombs and monuments to many famous Italians, including Dante (who is buried in Ravenna), Michelangelo, Machiavelli, Galileo, and Rossini. It also has frescoes attributed to Giotto and fresco cycles from the fourteenth century.

- Bargello: This museum contains many sculptures, including ones by Donatello (*David* and *Saint George*).

- Piazza della Signoria: Around this square are the town hall (il Palazzo Vecchio) and a loggia with sculptures including Cellini's *Perseus*.

    A stop at the Ponte Vecchio, the old bridge over the Arno, will provide you with a chance to see the latest styles in jewelry, and you will find many shops that sell leather goods throughout the city.

Milan lies 355 miles due north of Rome. It is Italy's gateway to Europe and its commercial center. Some of its major attractions are these:

- Duomo: The cathedral of Milan is a Gothic structure in marble famous for its roof, with its many pinnacles pointing into the sky.

- Galleria: This is a nineteenth-century passageway near the cathedral, now filled with shops, restaurants, and bars. It is a lively place to go to see and be seen.

- Santa Maria delle Grazie: Next to this church is the Dominican convent's dining room painted with Leonardo da Vinci's *Last Supper*.

- Brera: This is the major art gallery of Milan with works by Mantegna, Piero della Francesca, and Raphael.

As you look in shop windows, you will probably see examples of Italy's avant-garde design in furniture and clothing (see article 34, "Made in Italy"). And don't forget to sample these two famous dishes: *risotto alla milanese* (rice with saffron) and *costoletta alla milanese* (fried veal cutlet).

Dart across the north through some of these medieval and Renaissance cities: Verona, Vicenza, Mantua, and Padua.

In Verona, you should see a number of famous sites:

- Arena: These are the remains of the largest of ancient Roman amphitheaters, which could accommodate 25,000 spectators. As mentioned in other articles, operas are performed here during the summer.

- Piazze: The center of the town has two charming piazze: Piazza delle Erbe, a market square with stalls and awnings, and the Piazza dei Signori, with government buildings from the Middle Ages.

- San Zeno Maggiore: This church is a masterpiece of Romanesque architecture, with famous bronze doors with religious scenes that date from the twelfth century.

And, of course, you will be able to see what is supposedly the house of Juliet, the heroine of Shakespeare's play.

In Vicenza, you can see many buildings by the sixteenth-century architect Andrea Palladio, who worked in the neoclassic style, adapting Roman and Greek elements. These include:

- Teatro Olimpico: This theater, which is considered one of the finest in existence, was based by Palladio on theaters of antiquity.

- Corso Andrea Palladio: The Corso is the main street of Vicenza, and it has several palaces by Palladio, including the Palazzo Thiene.

In Mantua, or **Mantova**, you can see these sights:

- Palazzo Ducale: This ducal palace, the home of the Gonzaga rulers of Mantua, was built largely in the sixteenth century and is sumptuously decorated. Next to it is the Castello, which contains famous trompe-l'oeil frescoes by the Renaissance artist Andrea Mantegna depicting the Gonzaga court.

- Palazzo Te: This summer palace was designed by Giulio Romano, a follower of Raphael between 1525 and 1535 and has rooms frescoed by the artist, including the Giants' Room, showing colossal giants trying to reach Olympus.

Padua, or **Padova**, has these famous sights:

- Basilica del Santo: The basilica is a center of pilgrimage and devotion in honor of Saint Anthony, a Franciscan who died near Padua in

1231. Outside is a famous equestrian statue (1447) by Donatello of the military commander Gattamelata.

- Scrovegni Chapel: This chapel contains the most famous fresco cycle by the fourteenth-century Florentine painter Giotto. The cycle shows lives of the Virgin and Christ.

Your roamings have now taken you to one of Italy's most romantic cities: Venice, or **Venezia** (165 miles east of Milan). There you will have to leave your car and take a **vaporetto** or **traghetto** to get around the city's waterways. Many of the sites in the city date to the Middle Ages and Renaissance, when the city was a major sea power in the Mediterranean. On your list of places to visit should be these:

- Basilica di San Marco: This church, built from the ninth to the fifteenth century, reflects an eastern Byzantine style, with mosaics and marble decorating its five portals. Inside are more gold mosaics and the *Pala d'oro,* an altar covered with jewels and enamels.
- Palazzo Ducale: Next to the church on the famous piazza is the Gothic palace of the doges, the rulers of Venice.
- Canal Grande: On a trip along the Grand Canal, you can see many elegant palaces, many in a Gothic style. These include the Ca d'Oro (1440), which was once gilded all over.
- Accademia delle Belle Arti: This museum is a treasure house of works painted by Venetian masters, including Giovanni Bellini, Carpaccio, Giorgione, Titian, and Tintoretto.
- Scuola di San Rocco: This sixteenth-century building has a series of fifty-six canvases by Tintoretto depicting religious scenes.
- Murano: This is one of the islands in the Venetian lagoon famous for its glass and glass blowing.

Of course, many tourists take a ride on a gondola and listen to the serenades of the gondoliers. You can also get the flavor of the city by merely wandering along the back canals, encountering artisans and antique shops.

Upon leaving Venezia, one can chart a course toward the south, to Bologna, 94 miles from Venice and 227 miles north of Rome. Bologna is renowned for its cuisine, and its region of Emilia-Romagna has produced some of the best and most creative of Italian dishes, such as **tortellini** (filled pasta in the shape of rings), prosciutto, and parmesan cheese. Other than the restaurants, there are many things to be seen:

- Piazza Maggiore: This piazza is the center of city life. There is the church of San Petronio, one of the impressive, imposing Gothic structures with powerful sculptures by the Sienese artist Jacopo della Quercia. Off the piazza is the famous *Fontana di Nettuno* (Fountain of Neptune), considered one of the loveliest sixteenth-century fountains.

- Pinacoteca Nazionale: This museum contains paintings by famous local artists of the Baroque era such as Guido Reni, Annibale, and Ludovico Carracci.

As you stroll through Bologna, you will walk under the many arches that cover the sidewalks, forming a series of galleries and giving the city its unique character.

By now, you may need a break from sightseeing. Drive southeast to Rimini for a swim. The Adriatic coast has many vacation resorts that are often crowded with Italians and foreigners in the summer.

As you drive southward along the coast of the Adriatic Sea, stopovers in Ancona, Pescara, and Vasto will help you discover where the natives spend their vacations. The shore is outstanding and the food heavenly and more distinctive than in any other part of Italy. You may choose to drive inland to experience lovely landscapes dotted with mountains and valleys through the Molise province. A quick stop at Campobasso, the regional capital, will yield the visitor a chance to rub elbows with a warm, robust Italian character who clings to the past as well as the future. Foods such as scarmozze mozzarella, local wines, olive oil, pasta, meat and fish dishes, salumi and cheeses, and potato bread are characteristically Molisano. Natural spring water flows freely in the **sorgenti** and is always chilled naturally, even during the summer months. Air pollution is unheard of in this area and Italians from Rome and other cities spend their summer **vacanze** in this unspoiled spot.

Now head west back to Rome, a city that taxes a tourist's energy with its many sites to visit: ancient ruins, religious monuments, Baroque churches, and modern sections. Here are just a few highlights:

- Roman Forum: This was the center of ancient Rome, and you can see remains of various temples, the Roman Senate, and the Arch of Titus, built in A.D. 81 to celebrate the emperor's victory in Jerusalem. Nearby is what is perhaps the symbol of Rome, the Colosseum. Opened in A.D. 80, it could hold 50,000 spectators and was used for entertainment, mainly gladiator and wild animal fights.

- Campidoglio: This piazza near the Forum was designed by Michelangelo. On the right side is the city hall of Rome and on the left are the Capitoline Museums, with major pieces of ancient sculpture such as the Dying Gaul and the Capitoline Venus, as well as a painting museum with Baroque masterpieces.

- Pantheon: This temple, now a church, is perhaps the best preserved of Roman monuments. Its cupola with an opening at the center is considered a masterpiece of engineering.

- Piazza Navona: One of the most pleasant squares in Rome, it is built on the site of an ancient Roman stadium where races were run, hence its large oval shape. It has a fountain by the seventeenth-century artist Bernini.

- San Clemente: This basilica is in "layers," with remains of a fourth-century temple, fragments of frescoes from the eleventh and twelfth centuries, mosaics from the same period, and frescoes from the Renaissance, at different levels of the building.

- Villa Borghese: This magnificent seventeenth-century building contains major works of art, including paintings by Baroque artists such as Caravaggio and Bernini (including his sculpture *Apollo and Daphne*) and Canova.

- Vatican: This independent state, the smallest state in the world, is the heart of the Roman Catholic Church and the home of the pope. The Basilica of Saint Peter's, built over the tomb of the first pope, Peter, is one of the largest and most magnificent structures in the world, 610 feet long and 151 feet high (390 feet high at the center of its dome, which was a creation by Michelangelo). The adjoining Vatican Museums are a gigantic series of museums. They include the *Cappella Sistina* (Sistine Chapel) with ceiling frescoes of Old Testament scenes by Michelangelo and his *Last Judgment* on a side wall; the Stanze di Raffaelo, rooms frescoed by Raphael including *The School of Athens;* a museum with Greek and Roman sculpture; and a painting museum.

- La Scalinata di Spagna: This grandiose stairway built in the eighteenth century has 137 steps. It is a gathering place for Romans and tourists and is in the heart of the chic shopping area of Rome.

An obligatory site for tourists is **La Fontana di Trevi.** Although built in the eighteenth century, this monumental fountain is Baroque in style, with a figure representing the ocean in a chariot being drawn by sea horses. Tourists, of course, want to throw a coin into the fountain to be sure to come back to Rome. With their left-over coins, tourists can sit on the Via Veneto and buy a drink and watch Romans and tourists from other countries go by.

Continue your trip south, making a stop at Cassino and the abbey at Montecassino. The monastery is perched on the hilltop overlooking the valley with its spectacular views of the surrounding countryside. Here you will see the monastery established by Saint Benedict in 529 A.D., which is the cradle of Western modern civilization. The monks who lived there collected the major Greek and Roman manuscripts of the Classical Period, and transcribed them in artistic form for future generations. Kings, Popes, poets, and other prominent figures from all over the world have come to Montecassino to admire the art in its museum, the rococo architecture, and the melodic tones of the Gregorian Chants.

Now keep driving southwest to Naples, **Napoli**, 135 miles south of Rome. According to an old saying, **Vide Napoli e poi mori** (See Naples and then die), you haven't lived until you have seen Naples. Unfortunately the city is known for its poverty, but even this is out-weighed by the resourcefulness and cheerfulness of its citizens in getting by. Naples is situated on a spectacular bay. If sitting by the Mediterranean, eating superb fish dishes, and listening to songs is not enough, there are other things to do and see in the city.

- Certosa di San Martino: This monastery on the top of a large hill called *Vomero* provides the most famous view of the city and bay.
- Castel Nuovo: This "new" castle was built in 1282, when Naples was ruled by the Angevin dynasty from France. A triumphal arch in the Renaissance style, built in 1467 from designs by Francesco Laurana, bears the arms of the Aragonese rulers of the period.
- Museo e Gallerie di Capodimonte: In a royal palace of the eighteenth century, this museum houses paintings as well as porcelains in the elaborately decorated style called Capodimonte.

- Museo Archeologico Nazionale: This museum is one of the most important in the world for Greek and Roman antiquities.

Of course, one of the major remains of antiquity can be visited in the Bay of Naples: the ancient Roman cities of Pompeii and Herculaneum buried by the eruption of Mount Vesuvius in A.D. 79. You can also hire a guide to visit the top of Mount Vesuvius itself, which has not erupted since the 1940s.

By now, you are probably ready again to relax from the hustle and bustle of cities, and Naples and its environs offer world-class views and world-renowned resorts, such as Sorrento and the islands of Capri and Ischia. A trip along the Amalfi coast, where the mountains meet the clear blue waters of the Mediterranean, is a never-to-be-forgotten experience.

A drive farther south to the tip of the peninsula leads to Reggio, Calabria, where the Tyrrhenian, Ionian, and the Mediterranean Seas meet. There you will want to walk along the **Lungomare Marina,** an elegant promenade offering views of Sicily, the Straits of Messina, and the ships crossing the straits.

Take your car on the ferryboat and cross the Straits of Messina to Sicilia, once the seat of the Italian government. Take the autostrade around the island and stop at Taormina, Catania, Siracusa, Agrigento, Trapani, Castellammare del Golfo, Segesta, and Palermo. Sample the local treats, which are numerous and delicious. The Sicilian cuisine is lauded with accolades by all who visit Sicily and taste its fine choice of foods. The ancient recipes and nouveau cuisines celebrate a marriage that is second to none. From fish to meat, vegetables to legumes, pasta to pizza, desserts to cous cous, gelati to granita, Sicily has it all and more. Pastry and cassata were born on the island, and the quality and sumptuousness cannot be matched anywhere. Shopping is a marvelous event in Palermo; this city is home to museums, shops, boutiques, churches, squares, and wonderful outdoor markets. The island particularly is noted for its Greek ruins, which can be seen throughout the land. Beautiful and inviting beaches are a plus all around the island, where swimming is most enticing.

On the northwest coast, as you go through Palermo, the capital, there are more sites of interest.

- Palazzo dei Normanni: This immense palace, which is the seat of the Sicilian Parliament, was built in 1132 by the Norman kings of Sicily, although it has been remodeled several times over the centuries. Most interesting is the Palatine Chapel, built between 1130 and 1140, with excellent examples of Arab-Norman decoration, including mosaics.
- Catacombe dei Cappuccini: These catacombs offer one of the more bizarre sights: 8,000 corpses hanging in various positions.
- City Center: Three linked piazzas preserve the atmosphere of old Palermo: Piazza Bellini, Piazza Pretoria, and Quattro Canti.

And you can make a rest stop at Taormina, another world-famous resort, with a view of Mount Etna and the sea.

And on to Sardinia! You can get there from Genova, Civitavecchia, Naples, Palermo, and Trapani. This picturesque island is ready to be discovered. Relax on the beaches of fine sand of modern **Costa Smeralda.** Return to the Bronze and Iron Ages while standing in admiration in front of the numerous and massive prehistoric towers called **nuraghi.** Visit the pleasant metropolis of Cagliari and the partially submerged town of Nora. Listen to the sounds and voices of the inhabitants of Nuoro speaking a dialect very similar to Latin. And find the small treasures of old and modern times scattered throughout the island!

This whirlwind tour actually has left out many more interesting places than it mentions. Many of the historical and picturesque places in between the big cities have not been described. To get more information on cities such as Pisa (with its leaning tower and cathedral), Lucca (with its old walls), Como (on the lake of the same name), Portofino (the chic resort near Genoa), Orvieto (with its Gothic cathedral and fine wines), Monreale (with its mosaics), Urbino (with its Renaissance palaces)—to name just a few—you might want to refer to books such as L. and A. Gardiner's *Italy: Trip Planner & Guide* and *Regional Guides of Italy; Florence & Tuscany,* by Laura Raison; *Umbria, The Marches & San Marino,* by Christopher Catling; and *Naples & Campania,* by Martha Pichey; all published by Passport Books, a division of NTC Publishing Group.

31. THE KITCHEN

La cucina (kitchen) is revered as the most important place in the house. Despite its humbleness, it is the heart and pulse of the Italian home. This is the place where great dishes—both plain and elaborate—are prepared; where love results in a perfectly executed recipe for a cherished family member or friend.

La cucina is also the hub of Italian family life. It is the place where household members first meet in the morning to exchange greetings for the day. It is the place where **la famiglia** (family) enters when everyone comes home at the end of the day; the place where the children drop off their books after school as they enter the house. It contains the table where the mail is left by a family member after it is delivered, often placed next to a fruit bowl containing fresh fruit and alongside yesterday's newspaper. A section of the counter may accommodate several types of bread ready to be served at dinner. *La cucina* often serves as the place where informal company is entertained with all sorts of goodies and **pietanze** (snacks) and coffee and cake or cookies. It is the place where conversation is conducted and important decisions are conceived over **una bella tazza d'espresso** (a good cup of demitasse).

In short, *la cucina* is a spacious and comfortable room in most Italian homes where much of a person's life is lived and much of a mother's love is limitlessly given to her family and her friends.

32. THE LANGUAGE

The history of the Italian peninsula is complex and intricate as a result of Italy's geographical position in the middle of the Mediterranean.

Throughout the centuries, people from many diverse ethnic groups have come to Italy and have left visible traces of their presence: physical, cultural, and linguistic.

With the collapse of the Roman Empire, Latin lost its predominance as the universal language of Europe, and its offshoots—the Romance languages— gradually developed. Time, conquests, and the movement of peoples affected the various languages spoken on the Italian peninsula.

The new forms of speech, with their local characteristics, gave Italy its dialects. Neighboring towns spoke differently and with varying rhythmic cadences. Only in modern times have radio, television, telephone, and mass media helped the Florentine dialect reach a dominant role as a standard language. Dialects have not disappeared completely, and people resort to them when speaking with **paesani** (people from the same area) or close family friends.

Dialects give people a sense of identity and an attachment to culture and traditions about which they can feel proud. What dialects do people in the various regions speak? Here is some general information.

In the region of Aosta, in northwestern Italy, bordering France, the Valdostani speak a Franco-Provençal dialect. French is taught in the schools and is used in official documents, along with Italian. In neighboring Piedmont, the local dialect also intermixes with French:

T'ses pcit, t'ses semplice,	(You are small, you are simple,
Priv d'ogni blessa . . .	Without any beauty . . .
Faita a boule . . .	Made like a mushroom . . .)

The dialects of Lombardy, in the north center of Italy, use vocabulary words left from foreign domination. The inhabitants of this region claim to be able to communicate with many tourists by simply speaking in dialect. The Trentino Alto Adige links Roman and German cultures—and dialects. The Venetian dialects are considered soft and musical; they reflect the wit and cleverness of the local people. A noticeable difference exists in the speech pattern of Friuli-Venezia Giulia; it is harsh in the "Alto Friuli" and melodious along the coast.

The dialect of Genoa and surrounding areas, on the west coast, has the tendency to drop the *r* when it is between two vowels. Here is an example:

Mae aieri i ea eio, aoa i e eio e aia. (Genovese)

Il mare ieri era olio, ora e olio e aria. (Italian)

(Yesterday the sea was calm; today it is agitated.)

In addition, the letters *v, b,* and *p* in standard Italian are transformed into *c* or *g*, which complicates the understanding of Genovese.

In the Emilia region, the dialects are **gustosi** (amusing) and very difficult to comprehend unless the listener is from the city of Bologna.

Tuscany is the cradle of the Italian language. Although it has its particular words and accents, Tuscan forms the basis of modern Italian. Its vernacular was nobilitated by Dante Alighieri, Francesco Petrarca, and Giovanni Boccaccio. The dialects of the Marche region are easy and clear and reflect the open and friendly character of its people. The language spoken in Umbria, a blend of Etruscan and Latin, is immortalized by Jacoponi da Todi and Saint Francis of Assisi.

The **romanesco** (the Roman dialect) is easily understood and made popular by cinema and television. When people ask about the Italian language or which is the best Italian, one could say that it is **la lingua toscana in bocca romana** (the Florentine dialect spoken by a Roman). The soft sounds of the florentine combined with the harsh utterances of the Roman give the Italian language its pleasant character.

The language of the Abruzzi and Molise regions is strong, harsh, and deeply expressive. It is characterized by the use of double consonants that bring it closer to the dialects of Lazio (around Rome) and Campania (around Naples) regions. Many words are accented on the last syllable and it is similar to the **pugliese** (Apulia region), but without the elongated and open sounds of the vowel *e*.

The Neapolitan dialect is vivid and expressive. It is known throughout the world for the beauty and deep feelings of its songs (**la canzone napoletana**). **Torna a Surriento, O sole mio, Funiculì Funiculà**, and **Mala Femmena** are some of the better-known tunes.

The proverbs of Basilicata express the courage and the strength of these old migrants: **Si no ma sci ne sciame, si no nun sciami mica!** (When you have to do something, do it!). In Calabria many names reflect their Greek origin.

The Calabrese dialect is strong and musical and has the tendency to substitute the Italian articles (**il, lo, la, i, gli, le**) with **u**: **U cani muzzica u strazzato** (Dogs only bite the poor).

The colorful Sicilian dialects have traces of Greek, Phoenician, Arabic, and Norman languages. Even though people from the North and Central Italy have difficulty in understanding them, the Sicilian dialects are vivacious and expressive. Here is how the poet Giovanni Meli manifests its delicate, refined, and Arcadian simplicity:

> **Dimmi dimmi, apuzza nica,**
> **unni vai cussi matinu? . . .**
>
> (Tell me, tell me, my little bee,
> where are you flying so early in the morning? . . .)

The Sardinian dialect is strong and mysterious like its people. It has a peculiar intonation and a harsh sound. Many linguists have studied it for its numerous guttural sounds and the use of *s* as a final letter.

> **Deus seu sa jippa de oru . . .**
>
> (I am your little golden girl . . .)

In the area of Alghero, in northwestern Sardinia, people speak Catalan, the language spoken in and around Barcelona, Spain, and every year citizens from the two cities exchange visits. Alghero became a Catalan colony in 1354 and has kept the language since this period of foreign domination.

33. LETTERS

Call me—**Telefonami** or **Dammi un colpo di telefono**—are the expressions often heard as a way of keeping in contact with people. In Italy cellular phones are very popular, and, as in many other countries, verbal communication may seem to be easier and more direct than written words. Nonetheless, fax machines, computer electronic mail, and the bulk of personal and business correspondence indicate that letter writing is still very much alive. In personal and business letters, there are some expressions that you may see. Typically the salutations and closings may sound quite flowery and overblown in contrast to the more direct style used in English-speaking countries.

Informal Letters

Salutations

Salutations of letters to friends and family members typically begin with **caro/cara** (dear) or **carissimo/carissima** (dearest).

> **Anna carissima**
> **Paolo carissimo**

Closings

The following are examples of informal closings:

Abbracci	(Hugs)
Un forte abbraccio	(A big hug)
Affettuosamente	(Affectionately)
Baci	(Kisses)
Baci cari	(Loving kisses)

Formal and Business Letters

Salutations

In the salutation of letters to men, the name of the person is preceded by **Egregio Signor,** followed by his professional titles if any (**Avvocato, Dottore, Professore, Ingegnere**).

Egregio Signor (Professore) Mario Merli,

In the salutation of letters to women, the name of the person is preceded by **Gentile Signora** or **Gentile Signorina,** followed by her professional titles if any (**Professoressa, Direttrice, Preside, Contessa, Baronessa**).

Gentile Signora (Dottoressa) Rosa Rossi

It is common to see abbreviations such as **Chiar.mo, Ill.mo,** which roughly translates as "most illustrious."

The following formula is used in writing to businesses:

Spett.le Ditta (name)

Closings

Closings often sound very flowery. Here are some examples.

Con i più deferenti ossequi,	(Deepest respects)
Voglia gradire i sensi della mia profonda gratitudine,	(Please accept my expression of deepest gratitude)
Gradite i nostri più cordiali saluti,	(Accept our most cordial greetings)

34. MADE IN ITALY

Past and present are the catalysts, the triggers, and the creative imagination of Italians. Surrounded by the splendor of the past visible in every aspect of today's life, Italians are propelled into the future by their competitive spirit. Their ingenuity, love for life, and desire to compete have created an "exploit" of the "Made in Italy" stamp as a sign of excellence and elegance in quality and craftsmanship throughout the world.

Interior Design

Italians' art of elegance is reflected in the production of ceramic tiles, porcelain, marble ornamentation, wood flooring, vivid fabric and textiles, plastic laminates, and furniture design. Individual talents have flourished and gotten the attention world over with their handiwork and production techniques. They combine aesthetic views with functional purposes. Antique creations are reinterpreted and reproduced in a variety of patterns in wood, stone or metal. Furniture, colors, textures, light, and room interiors come together to give the viewer an authentic vista of the Italian Way of Life.

Crafts

Tablecloths, centerpieces, and placemat sets are as varied, colorful, delicate, and eye-catching as the political, cultural, and social diversity of each Italian region. Bedspreads, towels, napkins, shawls, and draperies display patterns of designs filled with the stories of local folktales. They are hand-embroidered and are still part of the trousseaus of Italian brides. The art of lace-making is both traditional and modern and very popular in today's Italy.

Companies such as Bassetti, Somma, Frette, Zeta, Tessilarte, Pratesi, and Borbonesi have made the Italian textile industry known throughout the world.

Murano Glass

Murano is a small island in the Venetian lagoon that is home to artisans and glass masters. They have perfected the glass-blowing technique and developed the famous **vetri di Murano.** They have achieved acclaim for their fine crystal and glassware. Stained-glass windows, chandeliers, figurines, crystal jewelry, and knickknacks in glass are fine examples of their artistic production.

Fashion

The "Italian look" refers to the distinctive fashions created by designers such as Giorgio Armani, Laura Biagiotti, Capucci, Fendi, Gianfranco Ferre, Krizia, Valentino, and Gianni Versace. Armani creates a soft, loose, and elegant look that allows the body to define itself.

Valentino designs are elegant, striking, and sexy; Biagiotti is elegant and feminine. Fendi is bold and dramatic. Capucci, the Michelangelo of fashion, represents the culmination of style and grandeur.

The Italian shoe industry has given the world designs that combine classical and modern styles. Superb leather and workmanship plus creativity have given the Italian shoemaking industry its distinctive style. Beltrami, Botticelli, Carrano, Ferragamo, Gucci, and Magli have emerged as the big names of Italian footwear. Handbags, briefcases, gloves, boots, and leather coats find their distinction in the Venetian, Florentine, or Neapolitan styles.

Italians also manufacture sleek, elegant, fast cars and motorcycles. Alfa Romeo, Bugatti, Ferrari, Fiat, Lamborghini, Lancia, Maserati, and Moto Guzzi all symbolize style and grace.

❁

35. *MA LEI NON SA CHI SONO IO!*

The most popular expression in the Italian language today could be easily identified as **Ma lei non sa chi sono io!** (You don't know who I am! [mah lEH-ee nohn sAH key sOH-noh EE-oh]). It is used everywhere and by anybody claiming to be important and powerful, with ties to people in high places. It comes in a burst of anger and frustration during a personal confrontation with individuals who dare to disagree with us or who are stepping on our toes in some way. The tone of the voice, the body language, and the excited use of hands and arms create a symphony that loudly and clearly carries the message of "Hey, you! Don't mess with me!"

The expression is also used jokingly with friends to poke fun at them and to be forgiven for silly behavior.

The person under attack may not ignore the verbal explosion and may quickly reply, **"Ma chi si crede di essere!"** (Who do you think you are! [mah key see crAY-deh dee EHs-seh-reh]). There will be a crisscross firing of the expression *Ma lei non sa chi sono io!* that will bring about the most colorful display of hand gestures, which may attract the attention of passersby. The verbal dispute usually ends with a handshake because both parties realize that they are trying to bluff the opponent with a fictitious show of strength.

36. *IL MALOCCHIO*

Il malocchio, or as it would be referred to in English, the "evil eye," is an everyday part of the southern Italian way of life. Ask any Italian who suffers from a headache, nausea, or grogginess or one who simply has trouble concentrating on even the simplest of topics, and the person will blame it on the *malocchio*. A sure sign of the *malocchio* is when the victim yawns in an uncontrollable manner.

The *malocchio* is not permanent. It can be removed if the correct incantation is uttered while a simple rite is performed. Though the rite may vary from **paese** to **paese** (local area), the ultimate effect is the same: relief. Sometimes the relief is almost immediate. Sometimes, however, achieving the desired result will require the rite to be performed several times, with the suffering gradually subsiding within an hour or so.

The rite may be performed in any one of several ways, depending upon the region of Italy to where your roots can be traced. From central to southern Italy, the rite includes the following elements: water, table oil, scissors, a tablespoon, and a soup dish. Water is poured into the dish, to the halfway mark. Prayers are said silently by the person performing the rite. The ritual performers then suspend a tablespoon of table oil above the dish of water and dip their index finger into the oil. Then they drop droplets of oil into the dish of water and analyze the clusters of droplets to determine the severity of the *malocchio* or if, indeed, the victim truly is suffering from *malocchio*.

The clusters and formations of oil beads (sometimes referred to as eyes) can determine if a male or female is the perpetrator of the "overlooking" that was the source of the *malocchio*. "Overlooking" can occur when someone says bad or evil things about someone, hence, *malocchio*, with an evil eye. "Overlooking" can also occur when someone speaks well of another incessantly and profusely, resulting in the victim getting a headache or another manifestation of *malocchio*.

After the performers of the ritual analyze the oil beads, they use scissors to cut into the beads to separate and dissipate them while they utter more incantations. The cutting of the oil beads (eyes) eradicates the *malocchio*. Their role in the destruction of the *malocchio* makes the scissors an important implement in the Italian home. Usually scissors are placed above a doorway in the home as a warning to the *malocchio* that if it attempts to enter, it will be destroyed. After the performers of the ritual cut the *malocchio*, they apply the oil mixture with their right thumb in the shape of a cross on the forehead of the victim in three different places.

There are other forms of the rite as well. In Bari, a sufferer is asked to calmly sit as the ritual performer places his or her right hand on the victim's forehead and forms a series of crosses with the right thumb. Prayers are said silently while the ritual performer periodically places his or her right fingers in a glass or dish of water and applies the moistened hand to the forehead and hairline of the sufferer in a sweeping motion.

Still another method is performed with a soup dish half-filled with table oil. After the ritual performers say some prayers silently, they drop several grains of wheat into the oil. If the grains drop to the bottom of the dish, there is no call for alarm since the *malocchio* is not present. However, if the grains remain afloat, it is a case of the *malocchio*. The floating grains must then be pierced several times with a pin to break the *malocchio*. If the grains continue to float, the *malocchio* has not been vanquished, and more piercing is performed until all of the grains sink to the bottom.

There are some surefire precautions that one may take to avoid getting *malocchio*. A person may wear a horn or a number 13 pendant around his or her neck or carry either of these symbols on his or her person. The number 13 is a sign of good luck in Italy. Therefore, its use is valued in prevention of *malocchio*. Today sporting such good luck paraphernalia is considered stylish, and many people wear jewelry that is in the shape of a horn. For the victim of a severe case of *malocchio*, a red horn is doubly appropriate since the color red wards off the "evil eye."

This power of the color red explains why Italians will tie a red ribbon to a baby carriage or a red bow around the steering wheel post of the new car. The answer is simply **Contro il malocchio** (protection against the "evil eye").

But why is *malocchio* associated with a baby carriage? Ask yourself what passersby do when a baby carriage is wheeled past them. They stop the carriage and admire the innocent contents: the baby. Modest praise such as **Che bellina** or **Che preziosa,** followed by touching the child, or lightly pinching the baby's cheek, should be all that is necessary to pay homage to the child. However, to some, only a litany of praises will suffice to express their delight with the child. When such accolades are profusely pronounced, although meant for good and not evil, there is fear that *malocchio* might result. And so the concerned parents place their trust in the red bow on the carriage to come to the aid of the defenseless child.

Jealousy and envy also have a connection with *malocchio*. Picture yourself driving a shiny new car down a street in your neighborhood while your neighbors watch. Do each of them sincerely congratulate you or wish you to have good luck and mean it? *"Malocchio!"* The red bow serves its noble purpose: *"Contro il malocchio!"*

There is also a ritual when an Italian moves into a new house or a new apartment. The first person entering must carry in the following things: a broom, a can of olive oil, salt, and scissors. The broom symbolizes a clean house and having the ability to sweep out evil. The salt is believed to have the power to stop evil or dispel it when it has entered a home. The salt must be sprinkled in every room and in every corner to drive out evil, which may hide even in the corners of a home. The oil and scissors are there to provide assistance if the *malocchio* comes.

One may only learn to remove the *malocchio* at one precise moment during the year. This is exactly at midnight on Christmas Eve. The power to remove the *malocchio* is awesome and is regarded as important in the Italian community. If you possess this knowledge, you must be prepared to be called on the telephone or have your doorbell rung at any moment as sufferers from *malocchio* or their family members ask for help to remove the discomfort quickly.

❸

37. M'ARRANGIO

Italy sits at the center of the Mediterranean Sea and for centuries has been at the crossroads of commerce, communication, and conflicts among the various people bordering its banks. The marks of centuries of invasions, domination, and mixing of peoples from different cultures are visible throughout the country on the facade of the buildings, the physical appearance of people, language, costumes, culture, and traditions. Italians have always faced adversities and have developed a strong survival instinct. When we scratch the surface of the glaze that beautifies the external aspects of the life of the rich and famous, we discover the everyday world of the simple people engaged in the struggle of daily existence. Many of these people are educated but unemployed. Many receive neither welfare nor any other public assistance. Some have a meager pension, others go through the day hoping to find a job, any job. They are generous and have the desire to be seen as respectable and productive members of a society that is desperately trying to face the plague of unemployment and inflation. These people will always answer with a smile, ''M'arrangio,'' when asked how they support themselves and their families. This old expression, borrowed from French military jargon, reveals the internal sadness that grips the heart of any Italian compelled to make ends meet. Soon after World War II, in order to satisfy the family's immediate needs and placate hunger, mothers picked wild dandelions to eat;

fathers and brothers collected metal scraps, fixed caldrons and broken dishes and chairs in exchange for a piece of bread, some pigskin, or oil and beans.

M'arrangio, may mean "I improvise." Thus an empty city road corner may give an opportunity to make some money. Someone may put on a cap and become a nonauthorized parking lot supervisor, and you can rest assured that your car will not be touched by anyone!

M'arrangio alla meglio means "I'll do the best I can" and may be uttered by delivery people, occasional messengers, and all-purpose helpers. With a flare, a young Neapolitan may, rain or shine, open up an umbrella and rent its services by escorting people across the street, to the bus stop, or to the train station. Another may open a shop near city hall and help passersby fill out applications and government papers for a few **lire. M'arrangio all giornata** means "I live from day to day." People may become "specialized" workers for a day in workshops, offices, or any other place that will give them the opportunity to make a few *lire.* Some may even become the assistant to the assistant doorman. However, *M'arrangio* can also have a negative connotation, especially when it is accompanied by a rotating hand gesture with the fingers moving in a circular motion as if to grab something. Said in this way, it may indicate "I support myself by stealing." *M'arrangio* is the motto for many members of the society, particularly in the central-southern and island areas where there is more unemployment. The verb **arrangiarsi** summarizes an attitude that helps people manage through hard economic times.

38. MEALS AND MEALTIMES

Meals do not just provide sustenance in the Italian way of life, but they can require as much effort as do great feats of athletics. This may seem to be somewhat of an exaggeration, since ordinarily one would not expect to find meals compared to sport. However, like a sport, meals require much preparation and time to be spent in readiness for the major event.

A holiday meal in an Italian family would begin with **antipasto** (appetizers): some cold cuts, **giardiniera** (pickled vegetables), several types of hard cheeses, dried sausage (sweet and hot), olives (black and green), and **grissini** (breadsticks). The first course might be a **stracciatella** (egg-drop soup) and progress to a pasta dish such as **lasagne,** baked macaroni, or a simple pasta such as **ziti** (large spaghetti-shaped noodles), **penne** (feather-shaped noodles), **rigatoni** (lined tubular noodles): never spaghetti on a holiday or a Sunday. There generally is more than one main course: several meats with gravy may be served (meatballs, sausage, grilled meats or **braciole**, and sometimes lamb or veal). Very often, these meats are precursors to several other entrees such as roasts (beef, lamb, or veal), chicken, and veal cutlets. To these are added the **contorni** (side dishes) of potatoes, vegetables, and salads, which could number five, six, or even seven or more. This cavalcade of sumptuous foods is followed by dessert, coffee, and after-dinner liqueurs.

Everyday meals will, of course, be less elaborate, but still may feature a pasta dish or a soup and a main course.

In Italy, one only need to travel in any direction for an hour or so to experience a very different cuisine. From north to south or east to west in Italy, a traveler may order a traditional pasta dish either with a cream sauce (northern style) or with a tomato sauce (southern style). In the east, the tomato sauce may be made with veal and lamb. In the west, beef is the preferred meat in a sauce.

Pastas vary according to size, cuts, shapes, and stuffings. In Florence, one would be remiss not to order **cannelloni** (a large pasta stuffed with meat) or **pappardelle** (lasagne-like noodles). Stop in Bologna and sample **lasagne, tortellini** (pasta filled with meat or cheese), or **tagliatelle alla bolognese** (pasta in a meat sauce made with butter, cream, ham, beef, celery, carrots, bacon, and onions). In the Veneto region, **pasta e fasoi,** (pasta with cannellini beans) is served up in a hearty portion. In Umbria, **spaghetti** is the specialty served under delicious sauces. Abruzzo boasts about its **fettuccine** and **spaghetti** recipes; Molise brings out **maccheroni alla chitarra** ("guitar" pasta, from the name of a wooden frame with metal strings on which it is cut), **fusilli** (spiral-shaped pasta), and **ravioli** (rectangular, filled pasta) recipes. Travel farther southwest and once in Naples pasta reigns: **ziti, bucatini** (tubular pasta), **cannolicchi** (short tubular pasta), **linguini,** and **spaghetti.** Apulia is a region of wonderful pasta dishes, among them **orecchiette** (little ears), **mignuice** (dumplings), **laganelle** (lasagna-like noodles), and **panzerotti** (a kind of ravioli). Still farther south one encounters Sicily and its magnificent pasta recipes utilizing home-made macaroni, as well as **gnocchi** (dumplings) and **cavatoni incannati** (pasta prepared with a rich sauce of tuna, mcat, or tomato, accompanied by zucchini or fried eggplant).

What is Italian cuisine? Why is it so popular? The secret is in the art of **Mamma Pincino: un pizzico qua, un pizzico là** (a pinch here and a pinch there). The variety of foods can accommodate everyone's tastebuds. The cuisine varies from the **fritti misti** (mix of fried fish) and **fegato alla veneziana** (liver) of Venice, to the **costoletta alla milanese** (breaded veal) of Milan, to the **bistecca alla florentina** (grilled steak) of Florence, to the **saltimbocca** (veal with prosciutto) of Rome. The list could continue on and on.

Nowadays, even lean cuisine is available in Italy. Some of this emphasis on the lean taps into traditional **casalinga** (home-style) cooking. This cuisine includes dishes such as **pasta e fagioli** (pasta and beans), **pasta con sarde** (pasta with fish), and **risotto con seppie** (rice with cuttlefish) and further complements it with **un bel bicchiere di vino** (a good glass of wine).

❁

39. MONETARY UNIT—THE *LIRA*

The **lira** is the basic monetary unit in Italy and its symbol is £. Its name derives from the Latin word **libra,** meaning "pound." The first Italian lira was minted in 1806. It was a silver coin that weighed five grams.

The Italian coins are issued in the following denominations: 50, 100, 200, and 500 lire. Those who are used to dollars will find Italian paper money rather fascinating. While dollars have the same basic color and the same size, Italian *lire* bills vary in size according to their face value and become larger as their value increases. They are very colorful and bear the pictures of important Italians.

Even though it is very hard to find one *lira* in circulation because of its minuscule value, two expressions with the word *lira* are still very popular: **non valere una lira** (to be worthless) and **non avere una lira,** to be penniless.

❁

40. NAVIGATING A BUILDING

Street signs in Italy are inscribed on marble or granite slabs that are affixed to the facades of the buildings at the corners or at the beginning and ends of roads. **Il palazzo** (building) reflects the architectural style of the time of its construction. In fact, the facade and interior may show evidence of having been built over the centuries. Alert passersby can have a lesson in history by simply admiring the structure of a building.

The entrance of the building leads to the ground floor, **il pian terreno. (Piano** means "floor" or "story.") **Il portinaio** or **la portinaia,** the concierge, takes care of the lobby, greets visitors and tenants, gives directions, and calls for the elevator. The next floor is **il primo piano** (the first floor, or U.S. second floor), which is followed by the **secondo piano** (second floor), **terzo piano** (third floor), and so on. **Lo scantinato** is the basement. Every *palazzo* has an inside courtyard.

The apartment's location is very important. An excellent apartment has a balcony and a beautiful view. The balcony is a place for outdoor meals in good weather. In some places, windows and balconies can be an interesting place for fast chats and gossip.

❁

41. NUMBER USAGE IN DIFFERENT SITUATIONS

Telephone numbers

Telephone numbers vary in their number of digits: they may have five, six, or seven digits. The numbers can be read individually or in groups. For example, 48567 can be read in two groups 48–567 (**quarant'otto cinquecento sessantasette**) or as individual numbers 4–8–5–6–7 (**quattro otto cinque sei sette**). Italians use area codes (**prefissi**) for different sections of the countries, as we do in English-speaking countries.

Addresses

In Italy, house numbers follow the street names; for example, Via Garibaldi, 8. Zip codes precede the name of the city; for example, 00056 Roma. A complete address would look like this:

Famiglia Rossi
Via Dante, 15
00056 Roma

Writing numbers

The number 7 is written with a line across the stem, and the number 1 has a serif (or sloping curve) at the top.

✿

42. ON STAGE IN ITALY

The sound of music echoes from the majestic amphitheaters and from the most isolated cloisters. These places are transformed into stages and present live performances that capture and delight the souls and senses of music lovers, both because of the quality of the masterpieces and the majesty of the surroundings.

The ruins of Italy's great past, her old cities, fountains, squares, palaces, and other monuments provide the natural setting for operas, festivals, and concerts. Indeed, the theatrical performances gain a backdrop that may be as dramatic as the work being performed. Visitors will not only please their senses and enrich their spirits, but also will increase their knowledge of Italian history. What is more beautiful, more spectacular, or more enjoyable than a trip to the Arena of Verona, the Baths of Caracalla in Rome, or the Theater of Taormina? They are special places that inspire reverence, where the past impacts on the present. Besides listening to the decibels and megawatts of the rock music that can shake from the foundations whatever has resisted the assaults of pollution and barbaric invaders, our youths can, in these places, experience classical music and dances. Concerts such as "Pop colossal" and operas such as "Aida" are presented at the Arena of Verona, while the Opera di Roma performs at the Baths of Caracalla. Lovers of the arts can embark on an educational tour that will bring them closer to the natural and cultural beauties of Italy from North to South, among sounds and images, songs and dances. The following is a tour of settings throughout the peninsula.

In the Veneto region, visitors can follow the winding roads through the **Ville Palladiane,** villas designed by the architect Palladio, whose use of classical elements inspired many architects, including some who worked in the United States. They will admire the seventeenth-century Villa Schio with the murals by Dorigny or view the Grimani Castle that dates back to the twelfth century. At Villa Trissino Marzotto and Villa Valmarana, the Venetian Soloists may enchant them with sonatas and concerts by Torelli, Vivaldi, Tartini, and Stradella. The Arena of Verona may be running the most successful performances ever held in this marvelous amphitheater, such as *Aida* by Giuseppe Verdi, **Cavalleria Rusticana** by Pietro Mascagni, **Pagliacci** by Ruggiero Leoncavallo, and **La Traviata** by Giuseppe Verdi. These operas are interpreted by the most famous Italian and international singers. The Roman Theater (**Il Teatro Romano**), smaller but not less glorious than the Arena, may stage comedies such as **Il Ventaglio** and **La Locandiera** by Carlo Goldoni and/or dances and jazz music.

The city of Venice will enchant the visitors with its open concerts in Saint Mark's Square, the evening gondola rides with music and singing, and the Film Festival (**Mostra d'Arte Cinematografica**), August–September.

In Tuscany, the green hills provide the backdrop for the performances at the magnificent Roman amphitheater in Fiesole, which overlooks the city of Florence. The **Balletto di Toscana** performs the ballets in the amphitheater, such as **Mediterranea** by the contemporary choreographer Mauro Bigonzetti. Another enchanting place is in Batignano, in the Maremma di Grossetto. There, in the eighteenth-century monastery of Santa Croce, there is an open-air festival called **Musica nel Chiostro** (Music in the Cloisters), where classical music can be heard.

Famous worldwide is the **Festival dei Due Mondi** (Festival of the Two Worlds), which takes place in Umbria, centered in the town of Spoleto. During the summer months, people come from many countries to attend music, dance, and theatrical performances.

In Rome, the festival **Roma Europa** and other musical events may fill the walls of the famous Roman villas overlooking the panorama of the Eternal City. The Baths of Caracalla will probably present the opera **Aida** by Guiseppe Verdi with chariots, horses, camels, and elephants. From the same stage, the ballet **Zorba the Greek** will bring the sounds and flavor of Greek music. Piano concerts are usually given at the Palazzo Farnese. Villa Massimo offers contemporary European dances, and musical exhibitions will be on the Gianicolo hill.

In Campania, in the hill town of Ravello, with its marvelous views of the Amalfi coast, there is the **Festival Musicale,** the Wagner festival at the end of June. It takes place in the very town where Wagner wrote some of his most famous music. The city of Naples has **Festa di Piedigrotta** in early September, with the world-famous **Festival della Canzone Napoletana** (Festival of Neapolitan Songs).

Sicily, of course, can offer ancient theaters for the sites of performances. The picturesque resort town of Taormina presents classical plays at **il teatro di Taormina,** renowned for its excellent acoustics. The Roman theater of Segesta, in cooperation with the **Istituto Nazionale del Dramma Antico** (National Institute of Classical Drama), may be the backdrop for comedies written by Plautus (250–184 B.C.).

At any time, at any place, you may come across a local festival. In town squares, folk groups in traditional costumes perform local dances accompanied by musicians. You may want to stand and watch, as you enjoy the stage that is Italy.

43. OPERA

Italy is the birthplace of opera. It is important to Italy's culture and soul. In most histories of music, the first opera is said to have been performed in Mantua in 1607. It was titled *L'Orfeo* and written by Claudio Monteverdi. Others argue that opera began in Florence with Peri's *Dafne* in 1598. In any case, we know that Monteverdi moved to Venice in 1613, and there opera experienced instant success with the opening of at least ten opera houses. And opera has been a major art form in Italy ever since.

There are two branches of opera: **opera seria** and **opera buffa** (serious opera and comic opera). With the evolution of instrumental music and the introduction of new instruments, the Italian opera reached its peak in the nineteenth century. Although opera today enjoys a resurgence from classical to even rock operas, the greatest ones still seem to have been written in the nineteenth century—the most prominent composers being Verdi, Rossini, Puccini, Donizetti, and Bellini.

The standard repertoire of opera houses around the world includes works such as Rossini's *Il Barbiere di Siviglia* (1816), Donizetti's *Lucia di Lammermoor* (1835), Bellini's *Norma* (1831), Verdi's *Rigoletto* (1851) and *La traviata* (1853), Puccini's *La Bohème* (1896) and *Tosca* (1900), to name a scant few by these major composers. Other composers also left classic works: Ponchielli's *La Gioconda* (1876), Mascagni's *Cavalleria rusticana* (1890), and Leoncavallo's *I Pagliacci* (1892).

In Italy today, more than twelve major opera houses boast of packed-house performances. These include the famous **La Scala** in Milan and the **San Carlo** in Naples. In Verona, the ancient Roman amphitheater, **L'Arena di Verona**, and in Rome the baths of Caracalla, **Le Terme di Caracalla,** are the sites for annual summer outdoor operas to sold-out crowds. Luciano Pavarotti with his extraordinary tenor voice carries on the tradition of a long line of Italian singers, including Caruso and Gigli, and he is sought after in opera houses throughout the world.

44. *IL PALIO*

Cor magis tibi Sena pandit (The city of Siena opens up its big heart to you) is written on the **Camollia** gate, which leads the visitors into town. In reality, the city offers travelers courteous hospitality in an environment of incomparable natural and artistic beauty. The spirit of the citizens of Siena is captured and embodied in the **Palio** (pAH-lee-oh), a festival and horse race held twice a year that features medieval costumes and flag twirling. This celebration pits the various neighborhoods (**contrade**) in a traditional competition. The spirit of the local neighborhood is strong in Siena. Each *contrada* is united as a family in an effort to bring home **il Palio,** a banner of silk cloth with an effigy of the Virgin and Child.

The origins of this centuries-old festival, which is celebrated every year on July 2 and August 16, are obscure. The celebration as we see it today was organized and given specific rules in 1632. Only ten of the seventeen *contrade* can compete in the horse race: seven by rotation and three by lottery.

The participating horses are not owned by the *contrade* but belong to fans whose only reward is to see their horses win the race at **il Campo,** the beautiful main city square. A city veterinarian checks over the horses and lets them run in groups of four in the square. The captains from the *contrade* select the ten horses that will be assigned to the *contrade* by lottery. The horses cannot be replaced. If a horse dies before the race, its *contrade* must withdraw. In the procession before the race, that *contrade* displays a dark banner while the pages carry the hoofs of the dead horse on a silver platter.

Finally, after days of preparation, the picturesque procession in medieval costumes headed by mace bearers, buglers, and standard bearers moves in the direction of the *Campo*. Important people from each *contrada* follow pages, drummers, and standard bearers who hold the banners of their *contrada*, twirl them around their bodies, throw them into the air, and catch them with astonishing prowess. The oxen-drawn cart with the banner bearing the image of the Madonna and Child moves about the square while trumpets blare, drums roll, and the bells from the city bell tower peal. When the parade comes to a halt, ten horses with their jockeys wearing the bright, colorful outfits of their *contrada,* come out, and the crowd is in a frenzy of expectation. It is just as important for a *contrada* to prevent a rival *contrada* from winning as it is to win itself. As a result, there are always suspicions that jockeys may be bribed to throw the race. This all adds to the expectation and excitement.

Three times the horses go around the 320-meter track. And a horse can be the winner if it crosses the finish line first, even if it is without a jockey. The winning *contrada* takes home the *Palio*, and in September for two consecutive Sundays, there will be a big dinner party in the *contrada*. The winning horse will have its hoofs painted with gold and will receive an extra portion of hay and sugar cubes.

While the **Palio di Siena** may be the best-known medieval pageant, other *Palio* contests take place in various Italian cities. The **Palio Marinaro** is a festival celebrated in Livorno (Tuscany). It is a boat race, and neighborhoods compete by rowing toward the old port of the city. In Arezzo, people perform a medieval joust, the **Giostra del Saracino,** the first Sunday of September. The participating four **rioni** (neighborhoods) select two knights who will compete for the gold lance. The knights accumulate points by hitting a wooden effigy of a Saracen, a puppet with open arms. The puppet's left arm holds lead balls and the right arm a shield. The knights have to charge the rotating puppet with their lances. They have to avoid being hit by the rotating metal balls while managing their horse and hitting the shield. *Il Palio Balestrieri* takes place the second Sunday in September in the town of Sansepolcro, near Arezzo. It is a crossbow shooting rivalry between archers of Gubbio and Sansepolcro dating back to 1461. In the city of Enna, Sicily, on August 14, the **Palio dei Normanni** takes place, a horse race commemorating the presentation of the key of the city to the Normans.

45. PEOPLE'S NAMES AND NAME DAYS

Buon onomastico! (Happy Name Day!) can be heard on a person's name day whether the name is Giuseppe, Lucia, Francesco, Antonio, Gennaro, Annunziata, Martino, Immaculata, or Carmela. Children are often named after a saint. A person's name day is the feast day of the saint after whom he or she is named. The name day may be of particular importance in a family who has received a favor from a saint and promised to name a child after the saint as a thank-you.

Names are often changed to diminutive forms as terms of endearment. For example, Giuseppe is appropriate for a twenty-year-old man, while Peppino is fitting for a teenager (Peppone is usually used for an elderly person). A teenage girl named Maria might be referred to as Mariella, Mariuccia, or Marietta.

Names are also combined, such as Pierluigi, Giancarlo, Rosamaria. Of late, Italians have developed a flare for new names: Katiushi, Walter, Mike. This phenomenon is largely due to the cultural exchanges provided by the media and by the return of Italians from other countries to their native land.

46. PHYSICAL DISTANCE AND CONTACT

Italians are demonstrative people and are given to touching while talking and patting the listener on the back when making an important point. The handshake they give is firm and confident. Both when walking or standing, people usually emphasize their points with gestures. (See article 26, ''Gestures.'')

During **la passeggiata** (the stroll), young people will place their arms around one another's waists or necks in a gesture of friendship and affection. It is common to see pairs of women who are friends or relatives walking holding hands. The distance between people in conversation is closer than in English-speaking countries. Just remember this is the norm!

47. *LA PIAZZA:* THE CENTER OF DAILY LIFE

Facciamo l'amore, non facciamo la guerra! (Make love, not war!) This is the typical Italian way of enjoying life. To the Italian, leisure time plays an important part of the day. Groups of people can be seen congregating in **la piazza** at the local café to have a cappuccino or gelato. *La piazza* is the heart of the town and is usually surrounded by the most important buildings: the church, the town hall, theaters, and cafés. The *piazza* is the meeting point for social encounters and the place for commercial activities such as the open market.

The *piazza* is the rendezvous for **la passeggiata** and the culminating point for the leisurely Italian stroll that is taken during **la serata** (early evening). This is the time especially when **i caffé** fill to the brim with the locals, who discuss politics, love affairs, and sports. It is a time to gossip about neighbors and to boast and brag about one's own exploits or those of one's family. Italians are careful to select the styles and fashions of clothing that they will sport at *la passeggiata,* since all are aware of the impressions they will make on each other. **Adesso é il tempo di ammirare ed essere ammirati!** (Now is the time to admire and the time to be admired!) Couples hold hands and throw coins in the fountain at the center of the square, thus keeping alive centuries' old traditions of well-wishing and good luck.

La piazza never sleeps and therefore never closes. Children may be kicking a soccer ball around and older people may be playing **bocce** (a game similar to lawn bowling) or cards, or reading newspapers while taking a few puffs of their favorite cigarettes or cigars. **I giovanotti** (the young people) ride into *la piazza* on the latest and most stylish **motorini** (mopeds) or in **macchine sportive** (sports cars).

The *piazza* is the political arena for anyone seeking political endorsements or exposure. It is the place for festivals, religious processions, and parades that give *la piazza* its cheerful function in Italian life. *La piazza,* in many ways, is the nucleus of Italian soul; it allows one to feel the pulse of the entire community and the essence of daily living.

48. POLITICIANS

Poised, educated, and well-dressed, the Italian politicians form a unique and peculiar social class. Versed in the arts of governing, they have mastered the Machiavellian concepts of fox and lion: cunning, opportunism, and aggressiveness. They are aware of the importance of their status achieved after seasoned years of preparation and hard work in the political arena and personify the ideologies of the numerous political parties in Italy. Several have a clearly defined **doctrina.** Others have borrowed concepts that have been kneaded into something subversive that, while keeping the substrata of the major ideological theories, have acquired new flavors and a touch of contemporary feelings.

Governments are formed from fragile coalitions of parties, which do not last long because of continuous and often futile internal feuds. Currently, there is no single leading party. (Through most of the postwar period, the Christian Democrats formed the leading party, even though it governed as part of coalitions.) And in recent years, many parties have changed names; for example, the Communist party is now ''The Democratic Party of the Left.'' New elections are being requested quite often, and after seeing and hearing politicians debate on television and radio talk shows, the majority of Italians tend to vote for the *person,* and not for his or her party. This was especially evident in 1994 with the formation of the **Forza Italia** party led by the industrialist and media magnate Silvio Berlusconi. (**Forza Italia** is the chant that fans use to encourage the Italian national soccer team during World Cup competitions.) It seemed not to be strong philosophical principles and political idealogy that led to the victory of Berlusconi in the 1994 elections, but rather the cult of personality and appeal generated by the use of the sport slogan.

At election time, politicians supply pompous speeches and rhetorical promises. Before elections, people may receive promises of jobs, gasoline bonuses, a ''social pension,'' or other enticements to vote for a candidate.

Today many Italians are unhappy with the performance and behavior of their elected officials. The people believe politicians have not worked for the betterment of the electorate or the country, but for their own personal interests. ''They are all for themselves'' and ''They think only about **la pagnotta** (their loaf of bread)'' are common remarks made by voters. Many believe that politicians are in league with criminal organizations such as **la camorra** in the area around Naples, **la 'Ndrangheta** in the Calabrian region, **la Sacra Corona** in Apulia, the **mafia** in Sicily, and the **banditi** in Sardinia.

Recently, a group of law-abiding citizens led by the magistrate Dr. Antonio Di Pietro have had the courage to investigate, indict, and prosecute several prominent political figures entangled in the scandal involving bribes (**tangenti**); a person receiving *tangenti* is an individual "on the take." The organized crime groups have responded by perpetrating unscrupulous and vindictive acts such as kidnappings, bombings, and murders of respectable prosecutors and people on police forces. In spite of this, the operation **mani pulite** (clean hands) reaffirms the strength and the courage of real democratic convictions. These investigations have led to the prosecution of several major politicians, including the former prime minister Craxi, and to a major housecleaning among the political classes. Berlusconi himself, threatened with being investigated for his industrial and political practices, resigned at the end of 1994.

Italians, thus, are seeking ways to have a more effective political system with more honest and effective leaders. One proposal is to form a federation based on the Swiss model. The Italian voting public has many important decisions to make as the country approaches the twenty-first century.

49. PROFESSIONAL AND CIVIC TITLES

Italians have the highest respect for those who are able to climb the ladder of success through hard work and education. They shower these individuals with titles and make them feel very important in the community and place of work. Many times the titles of **dottore** or **cavaliere** are freely given to anyone who is needed for favors. Neapolitans are masters in bestowing titles upon foreigners and acquaintances. They say them in jest and make another believe conversely that he or she is really important. **Don, donna** (master, lady) were used extensively by Sicilians in addressing people of importance or as a sign of respect for older people or strangers.

The formal titles of address—**signore, signora,** and **signorina**—are used when one is speaking to people who are not well-known to the speaker. Professional titles such as **dottore, dottoressa, avvocato,** and **professore** are used with university graduates. Titles of noble origins such as **conte** or **contessa** and religious affiliations are still in use. Italians love to have and use titles.

50. PRO LOCO

Visitors to Italy may buy travel guides and phrase books in an attempt to get information and make their Italian experience memorable and exciting. In Italy, every town has a history and a character that makes it unique. In their desire to share their cultural heritage with whomever shows an interest in their way of living, the inhabitants have created the Pro Loco organizations. Pro Loco (Latin, meaning "in favor of the place") organizes, sustains, and encourages cultural and artistic programs with the intent of promoting tourism and awareness of local culture and events. Pamphlets, maps, illustrative booklets, and calendars of events are part of the promotional packets distributed at the local Pro Loco offices. Information is provided by well-informed and concerned students and educators who are versed in several languages. Phone books list telephone numbers and addresses of local Pro Loco offices.

51. PUNCTUALITY

For the most part, Italians are quite punctual. Just go to church a half-hour before mass, or to a doctor's office a half-hour before appointments begin and note how many people are there waiting. For the theater or the opera, Italians are careful to arrive **puntualmente** (punctually) with sufficient time to chat and get comfortable to fully enjoy the performance.

But **le persone importanti si fanno aspettare** (important people arrive late). This is a common trend among young people. **Sono in ritardo, perciò sono importante** (I'm late, therefore I am important). Being late is an unspoken form of social status!

Office workers seem to be affected by **a domani** (till-tomorrow) syndrome, especially dealing with an inquirer who is looking for a quick response to his or her immediate needs. **Passi domani!** (Pass by tomorrow!) or **Si faccia vedere più tardi!** (Come back later!) may be the response. When things get tough and people begin to react in an angry manner, clerks, managers, or supervisors will spring into action by saying **Ma che c'è? Che le occorre? Mi dia qui! La servo subito!** (But what's going on here? What do you need? Give it to me! I'll take care of it right away!).

Italians accept this type of behavior and deal with it on a daily basis, even though many may express their frustration mumbling under their breath **Mannaggia la miseria! Ma qui nessuno fa mai niente!** (Darn it! Nobody does anything here!)

52. *LA RACCOMANDAZIONE*

Everyone needs a little help in order to be successful in life. A letter or a word or a recommendation may be the magic wand that opens many doors. **Ce l'hai una buona raccomandazione?** (Do you have a good recommendation?) **Qui ci vuole una buona raccomandazione.** (You need a good recommendation for this.) These phrases may be heard when one is making plans to apply for a job, enter a contest, or take an examination.

An Italian dictionary might define **la raccomandazione** as the situation where one person brings another person to the attention of a third party. This is done for the purpose of helping someone to be hired or obtaining favorable treatment. The agent must, of course, have some clout.

La raccomandazione may be part of the Italian folklore and its origins may be lost in the past, but it is very much present in today's society and may affect the behavior of many. Even when someone obtains a job solely based on personal merits, people whisper: **Ce l'ha fatta perché è raccomandato di ferro** ([chay lah fAHt-tah pehr-kay EH rah-koh-mahn-dAH-toh dee fEHr-roh], He made it because he had a very strong recommendation). It is a socio-economic phenomenon that works like a catalyst. *La raccomandazione* is usually remunerated with a gift or the famous **bustarella** ([boo-stah-REHL-lah], envelope containing an undisclosed amount of money as a kind of bribe). No one goes anywhere without *la raccomandazione* and it is understood that with it goes the honor of the person who gave it. Once *la raccomandazione* is obtained, one must uphold all the virtues extolled by it and not embarrass or disparage the contact's reputation with unsatisfactory behavior or unsatisfactory work ethics.

53. RELIGION

The major religion in Italy is Roman Catholicism. Although there are other groups of Christians, and Jews have been in Italy since before the coming of Christ, the greatest number of Italians are

Catholics. When you enter most homes, restaurants, offices, banks, or schools, you will see a crucifix affixed to a wall, a statuette of the Blessed Mother on a shelf, or a picture of the pope in the kitchen. An Italian will seldom say he or she feels well or that things are going well without suffixing the statement with **Grazie a Dio** (Thank God). Many Italians cross themselves before eating a meal or before leaving the house to go to work or school. When passing a church or a religious statue or shrine, they do the same and even recite a silent prayer.

If special favors or **miracoli** (miracles) are granted through the intercession of certain saints, or if special events such as apparitions occur, shrines are erected. Bouquets of flowers and lit candles are left by the faithful to honor the saint. Many towns hold processions on special feast days originating in **la chiesa madre** (the mother church of the town, often dedicated to the town's patron) proceeding through the main streets of the town, and returning to their point of origin. Italy has many famous shrines. Among these are the basilica of **San Francesco** (Saint Francis) in Assisi and the shrine of **Sant'- Antonio** (Saint Anthony) in Padua.

And churches seem omnipresent, particularly in Rome, which is the center of Roman Catholicism. The Vatican is an independent country located in Rome and is the home of the pope, the vicar of the Catholic Church. Italians pride themselves in the knowledge that **il Papa** (the Pope) is so closely associated with their country. In fact, in the modern era, most popes have been of Italian origin, and Italians have dominated the church's hierarchy.

Through its history as a nation, Italy has been closely connected to, and strongly influenced by, the Catholic Church. For instance, until recently, church law was accepted as part of the Italy's penal law. One example is that not until 1980 could married couples divorce in Italy. Many major national holidays are religious in nature and virtually all local town holidays commemorate particular saints' days.

54. RESTAURANTS

In Italy, restaurants can be divided in various categories. The type and size of the meal you want will dictate the kind of restaurant you choose. When a smaller meal is wanted, you only need to locate a **trattoria** for tasty foods. *Trattorie* are less expensive, less pretentious, and often family-run restaurants. **Primi piatti e secondi piatti** (first and second courses) are a daily mainstay. *Trattorie* can be found throughout Italy, from the smallest towns to the largest cities. Many offer a tourist menu with fixed prices. Such a menu typically includes a pasta dish followed by a salad, entree, coffee, and dessert. At these eateries, hungry patrons eagerly order **pizza quattro stagioni** (four seasons pizza), **minestrone** (vegetable soup), various pasta dishes, entrees such as **filetto di turbo** (turbo fish fillet) or **petto di pollo arrostito** (roasted chicken breast). Meals are topped off with desserts, which can range from **crostate** (fruit tarts) to **zabaglione** (egg-custard flavored with marsala), fresh fruit, or **macedonia** (fruit salad with liqueur) and the best **espresso** (strong coffee) or **cappuccino** (coffee with steamed milk) available anywhere on earth. When a special moment is to be celebrated or intimacy is sought after, a more sumptuous and extravagant meal is served in a **ristorante** (restaurant). Almost as numerous as *trattorie, ristoranti* can be found throughout Italy and range from the simple to the lavish. In general, items are *a la carte* and meal prices somewhat higher than at *trattorie*. Portions are fancier and smaller with quality at the forefront.

Tourists will note that restaurant hours may be different from what they are accustomed to. They open for lunch around noon or one o'clock, but may not open in the evening until seven thirty or eight o'clock.

55. *LO SCIOPERO* (STRIKES)

Sciopero! Sciopero! (Strike! Strike!) (shee-OH-peh-roh), people shout when their demands are not met by their employers or when they are requesting changes in their employment conditions. Peaceful demonstrations, shouting matches, and sudden work stoppages have marked the road to the Italian economic boom. Italians have made an art of it!

Panic and fear of being stranded anywhere and anytime rock the hearts and souls of Italians. Trains stop in the middle of nowhere. Nurses walk out of operating rooms. Postal workers close their windows while people are waiting in line. Restaurants do not serve food, and students cut classes in sympathy for the strikers, mindless of the ultimate results of their actions. The Italian word **sciopero** varies in tone and meaning. Its variations are almost poetic in scope, with many words to define the different types of strikes.

Lo sciopero articolato is called by sectors and programmed in such a way that work is stopped according to the expiration date of different phases of the union contract. **Lo sciopero generale** is a general strike, where most services shut down. **Lo sciopero a oltranza, a tempo indeterminato** goes on until all the demands by the workers are met by the employers. **Lo sciopero a catena** is characterized by a succession of work suspensions in different sectors with brief intervals between them to disrupt service. **Lo sciopero a scacchiera** is put into effect at different intervals by workers in different areas of production. **Lo sciopero a singhiozzo** is a wild-cat strike with short intervals of work. **Lo sciopero a sorpresa** is a spontaneous, uncalled strike that is not backed by the union. **Lo sciopero bianco** consists in the execution of work with extreme care according to rules and regulations to slow down production. **Lo sciopero selvaggio** calls for the alternate suspension of work in certain sectors of an industrial workplace in order to make it impossible to assemble the final product. **Lo sciopero di solidarietà** is in support of other striking unions.

Jokingly one says **È giorno di sciopero** on a day of vacation or a holiday. While strikes are part of the normal daily life of an Italian, they may seem strange and absurd to people from other places. **Informarsi bene** (be well-informed) is the only answer available to travelers in Italy to avoid being caught in the middle of *uno sciopero*.

56. SHOPPING

Shopping in Italy is an unforgettable experience. It can be challenging, tempting, nerve-racking and gratifying. Stores and merchandise have local, national, and international flavor. **I mercati delle pulci** (flea markets) may display centuries-old articles. **Le botteghe** (small shops) may have an array of local crafts whose manufacture has been passed down from generation to generation, and the modern shops allure the buyers with their **vetrine** (shop windows), sometimes filled with contemporary fashion exhibits.

Many stores have fixed prices, but others are prepared to be less fashionable and afford the opportunity to haggle. A good shopper should always examine the product for its quality and must not seem anxious to buy it. If the price is to come down, imperfections (whether real or imaginary) should be found. For example, the color is fading; the stitches are too far apart; the glass is not thick enough. Say **veramente non mi serve** (I really don't need it); the product is not an original; and the shop next door sells exactly the same thing at a lower price. A frown should also accompany the transaction.

Open markets are colorful and animated places. They are filled with the voices of shouting vendors trying to attract attention and to persuade potential buyers of the fine quality of their products. You may hear conversations like the following: **Come? Che prezzo hai? Ma sei pazzo! Ma che imbroglione! Avvolgilo e non farmi arrabbiare!** (What? What's your price? Are you crazy? What a con artist you are! Wrap it up and don't make me angry!) However, transactions are actually mostly cordial. Cash payments are preferred to personal checks and plastic cards. The most unusual form of shopping is that of **il cestino** (basket) dropped down by the housekeeper from a balcony to the street vendor below. The merchandise is placed in the basket, pulled up with a rope and unloaded, and the basket is then lowered with the money for the goods.

At the other end of the spectrum from the local markets are

the major department stores, such as UPIM and STANDA. These stores are located nationwide, from north to south. Of course, they offer a standardized, rather than a personalized, shopping experience.

Names of Stores

Italy has such a large variety of shops that it is helpful for the tourist to recognize names:

abbigliamento da uomo	men's clothes
abbigliamento da donna	women's clothes
alimentari	grocery store
bar	coffee and drinks shop
edicola	newspaper stand
enoteca	wine shop
farmacia	pharmacy
ferramenta	hardware store
fioraio	florist
fruttivendolo	fruit store
gelateria	ice cream parlor
giocattoleria	toy store
gioielleria	jewelry store
macelleria	butcher shop
mobilificio	furniture store
ottico	optical center
panetteria	bread bakery
pasticceria	pastry shop
pelletteria	leather goods shop
pizzeria	pizza shop

57. SIGNS

When you go to Italy, you will be surrounded by signs. Of course, many signs will use international symbols or may be in several languages, but others may be in Italian only. Here are some words that you may encounter on signs and with which it will be helpful for you to be familiar. They are useful for getting along in Italy.

Word	Meaning	Where Found
aperto	open	on store windows
binario	track	in train stations
cassa	cashier	in banks, bars
chiuso	closed	on store windows
chiusura settimanale	weekly closing	on stores
domenica	Sunday	
lunedì	Monday	
martedì	Tuesday	
mercoledì	Wednesday	
giovedì	Thursday	
venerdì	Friday	
sabato	Saturday	
donne	women	on bathroom doors
è pericoloso sporgersi	it's dangerous to lean out	on trains
fermata	stop	on bus stops
guasto	out of order	on machines
orario	schedule	in train stations
parcheggio	parking	on streets
piano	floor	in buildings
senso unico	one way	street sign
spingere	push	on doors
tirare	pull	on doors
uomini	men	on bathroom doors

Word	Meaning	Where Found
uscita	exit	in buildings
vietato	it is prohibited	on various street signs

58. *LO SPORT*

Sports are a way of life in Italy. Italian's love affair with sports manifests itself in passionate discussions about soccer, bicycle racing, skiing, boxing, and other athletic activities. Italian **tifosi** (fans) are very emotional in their display of feelings for **la squadra del cuore** (favorite team).

Il calcio (soccer) is a favorite national pastime. Children play soccer in the square, in open areas, in fields, and anywhere and everywhere there is an open space. Any soccer game offers an exuberant display of what **il tifo** (sports fanaticism) is. The most famous soccer players are talked about, revered, and put on pedestals as if they were demi-gods. They are imitated by **i pulcini** (Little League soccer players), who hope to make it to **la serie A** (the top Italian soccer league). Fans crowd into the stadiums on Sunday afternoons. Radios and televisions are tuned to the games while other activities come to a halt. **Forza, Roma! Forza, Milan! Forza, Napoli!** are cheers yelled by the excited spectators. Fans of each team hope to win **lo scudetto,** the coveted championship shield. On the international level, Italian teams have a good reputation. The national team, called **gli azzurri** (the Blues), have won three World Cup championships, second only to Brazil's four. They won in 1934, 1938, and 1982; they were in the semifinals in 1990 and the finals in 1994 (which they lost to Brazil in a shootout). They have also performed well in other international championships such as **la coppa delle coppe** (the super cup) and **la coppa dei campioni** (cup of champions). (See article 10, *"Calcio."*)

Il Giro d'Italia (eel jEE-roh dee-tAH-lee-ah), the Tour of Italy, and **La Milano-San Remo** (lah mee-lAH-noh sahn rAY-moh), the Milan-San Remo Race, are two of the most popular bike races in Italy. Athletes from all over the world compete for **la maglia rosa** (lah mAH-ly-ee-ah rOH-sah), the pink jersey, and the trophy. The names of Gino Bartali, Fausto Coppi, Francesco Moser, Felice Gimondi, and Gianni Motta are remembered for their strength, competitive spirit, and dedication to the sport and their fans. **Fare la volata** (to win the final sprint), **attaccare in salita, in discesa** (to attack uphill, downhill), **andare forte** (to run a strong race), and **tagliare il traguardo** (to cut the finish line) are expressions familiar to every fan.

Il ciclismo (cycling) is a sport of intelligence, physical fitness, and character. For this, the old and new champions are understood and remembered by their fans. *Il ciclismo* is made of dualisms, of opposite factions, of Coppisti and Bartaliani, Moseriani and Saronnisti. The fans spend hours waiting to see their idols flash in front of them for a few seconds only!

Italians have a great passion for fast-running cars. The cars zoom up and down the **autostrade** (highways) without paying much attention to the speed limit. Fancy cars such as **la Ferrari Testarossa** epitomize the dream car. **Il Circuito di Monza** (eel cheer-kOO-ee-toh dee mOHn-tzah) is to Italians what the Indianapolis 500 is to Americans.

Boxing also has its following in Italy. There have been several world champion boxers who were Italian, including Primo Carnero, the only Italian to hold the heavyweight title (winning it in 1933) and middleweights Nino Benvenuti (1967) and Vito Antuofermo (1979–1980).

Recently, in the Winter Olympics Italy's **Alberto Tomba** has won gold medals in the giant slalom. In 1992, Tomba won the season championship in the slalom and giant slalom as well. In the Winter Olympics, he took the gold medal in the giant slalom and the silver in the slalom. Tomba also won nine World Cup races. **Deborah Compagnoni** has won the super giant slalom. For the World Cup, in races held from November 1992 through March 1993 in Canada, Europe, and the United States, **Gustavo Thoeni** won four times. Italian fans are electrified by the success of their idols.

The importance of sports to Italians is proven by the many newspapers devoted exclusively to sports, which have a large readership. These include *La Gazzetta dello Sport* and *Il Corriere dello Sport*.

59. TELEPHONES

Telephones in Italy have two different rings. When the line is busy, the signal heard is a long too-too-too sound; when the line is free, the too-too-too sounds are short and quickly repeated. Public telephones are found in bars, cafes, and station terminals. Magnetic telephone cards, **gettoni** (tokens), or coins are needed to make a phone call. Clicking timers are in place at many telephone centers and the charges are set according to the number of **scatti** (clicks) marked by the timer.

People are very polite on the phone, especially when making calls to people's homes. The following is a typical example:

Il signor Bianchi: Pronto! Casa Rossi?	Hello! Rossi's residence?
La signora Rossi: Pronto! Chi parla?	Hello! Who's calling?
Il signore Bianchi: Sono il signor Bianchi.	This is Mr. Bianchi.
La signora Rossi: Buongiorno. Desidera?	Good day. What can I do for you?
Il signor Bianchi: Vorei parlare con Maria.	I'd like to speak with Mary.
La signora Rossi: Attenda un attimo, per favore.	Wait a moment please.

A local phone call is **una telefonata urbana.** Long-distance calls are **telefonate in teleselezione, interurbane.** International phone calls are **telefonate internazionali.** Phone calls to anywhere in the world can be made from any public phone. When tokens are used, a required amount of *gettoni* must be inserted before dialing the number. It is important to know that tokens are held in the slot until the recipient of the phone call says **Pronto!** (Hello!). The caller then presses the release button and allows the tokens to drop inside the machine to continue the call.

60. THE TERM *AMERICAN*

In Italy, the term **Americano** indicates a person from the United States, **Gli Stati Uniti.** *America* has become a synonym for the United States. The other countries from North America and South America are referred to by their individual names: Canada, Mexico, Colombia, Venezuela, Argentina, and so on. When an Italian immigrant living in the United States returns to Italy, he or she is referred to as **l'americano/a.** Someone coming from Canada is **canadese,** from Venezuela is **venezuelano,** from Argentina **argentino**, and so on. Old worldwide preoccupation with the United States and Americans continues to the present day. People are fascinated with the way of life of Americans. The expression **È un'americanata** indicates an extraordinary, often unbelievable event or an eccentric taste or behavior; for example, **Il ricevimento è stato un'autentica americanata** (The party was unbelievable).

61. TESTS

Students are tested in writing and orally from elementary school through college. A combined grade is the final mark for the class or course. Report cards are given quarterly. Final examinations leading to a high school diploma are national examinations. They are followed by additional exams, which include both oral and written parts, administered by a **commissione** (board of examiners) in the month of July. Only the *commissione* can award the high school diploma.

College examinations for a course are in many instances limited to a single final examination. Students may prepare for it for approximately five months. Many college courses do not require classroom attendance, but the students must obtain permission to take the examination from the course instructor.

Copiare (cheating) might be punished with expulsions and suspensions. Students are very clever in using the subtle art of deception especially during a written examination. It is almost a game, a challenge for the students to try to outwit the professors and **non farsi beccare** (not get caught).

62. TIME OF DAY

Official time in Italy is based on the twenty-four-hour clock. When the time is written in Italian, a comma is used between the hour and the minutes.

L'aereo parte mercoledì alle 15,30	(The airplane leaves on Wednesday at 3:30 P.M.)

Schedules, timetables, and the like always use the twenty-four-hour clock to avoid confusion. Italians, however, do not always use the twenty-four-hour clock in conversation.

L'Uffico Postale apre alle 9,00 (nove) del mattino.	(The Post Office opens at 9:00 A.M.)
La partita comincia alle 2,30 (due e mezzo) del pomeriggio.	(The game starts at 2:30 P.M.)

It is easy to figure out time on the twenty-four-hour system. Simply subtract 12 from the number.

16,25 is 4:25 P.M. (16,25 − 12,00 = 4,25)

Telling time in Italian is expressed with two different verbs: **è** for 1:00, noon, and midnight; **sono** for all other numbers.

Che ora è?	kay OH-rah EH	(What time is it?)
È l'una.	eh lOO-nah	(It's 1:00.)
È mezzogiorno	eh meh-tsoh-jee-OHr-noh	(It's noon.)
È mezzanotte	eh meh-tsah-nOHt-teh	(It's midnight.)
Sono le due.	sOH-noh leh dOO-eh	(It's 2:00.)
Sono le tre.	sOH-noh leh trAY	(It's 3:00.)
Sono le quattro	sOH-noh leh koo-AHt-troh	(It's 4:00.)

The conjunction **e** (*and*) is used to express the number of minutes after the hour.

Sono le tre e dieci.	sOH-noh leh treh ay dee-EH-chee	(It's 3:10.)

The phrase **e un quarto** and **e mezzo** are used to express fifteen minutes after the hour and half past the hour.

Sono le sette e un quarto.	sOH-noh leh sEHt-teh ay oon koo-AHr-toh	(It's 7:15.)
Sono le otto e mezzo.	sOH-noh leh OHt-toh ay mEH-tsoh	(It's 8:30.)

By subtracting the number of minutes to the next hour, the Italians express time after passing the half-hour point on the clock.

Sono le dieci meno venti.	sOH-noh leh dee-EH-chee mAY-noh vAYn-tee	(It's 9:40.)

Phrases like **Sono le tre e quarantacinque** (sOH-noh leh trEH ay koo-ah-rAHn-tah-cheen-koo-eh), It's 3:45, are becoming more popular with the use of digital watches and clocks.

❁

63. TRANSPORTATION

It is easy to travel throughout Italy: the country offers a network of modern highways, railways, and ferries. The **autostrade** (superhighways) like L'Autostrada del Sole cross the spine of Italy, linking north to south. Traveling by car is fast and direct. (See article 18, "Driving in Italy.")

Train services are efficient and reliable (except for strike periods, of course). They are commonly used by Italians. The Italian State Railway is called **Ferrovie dello Stato** (FS). For travel in Italy, tourists might consider buying one of the various kinds of Eurail passes. They might also consider purchasing passes available from the Italian State Railway. These include the BTLC "Go Anywhere" pass for first- and second-class travel and the Italian Kilometric Ticket, which is good for twenty trips or 3,000 kilometers (1,875 miles) of travel. Travel is permitted on Intercity, Eurocity, Rapido, and ETR 450 trains. Ticketholders traveling on the ETR 450, Italy's fastest train, must pay a supplemental fare, and they must have their tickets stamped at the ticket booth for mileage before boarding.

Ferry services link the mainland of Italy to Sicily and Sardinia. **Aliscafi** (hydrofoils) and other boat taxis are also available. Air services are provided by Alitali, ATI, and other airlines to every region and major city.

Transportation in and around the cities can be done by city and intercity buses. Maps are available of the city bus systems from tourist offices and at bus system offices. And in Venice, there is a system of **vaporetti** (boats). Rome and Milan have subways. On the street, the station entrances have a large *M* indicating **la metropolitana** (subway system).

☙

64. THE TWO FACES OF ITALY

The Center-North

Traditionally, the Center-North of Italy has been looked upon as the "productive" area of the country. Its geographical configuration has been a determining factor for its agricultural and industrial development. The mountain chain of the Alps in the North, while protecting the **Pianura Padana** (the Po River Valley) from the cold winds, provides enough spring water for several rivers and Po tributaries to make the valley very fertile. The Alps form a natural barrier that defines the boundaries with bordering countries. With their world-renowned slopes, they are also the focal point of the ski industry. The lakes and lagoons adorn the area in complete assonance with the flora and fauna of the surrounding landscape. The high mountains descend in graceful curves forming green hills, which gradually slope down to the winding Po that lazily flows toward the Adriatic Sea. These plains, rich and full of life, are gemmed with the precious evidence of the laborious and incessant productive creativity of their inhabitants. From country villas to historic city centers, where modern ways of life pulsate with work and commerce, the indelible memories of a glorious past fill the present. Sleek skyscrapers tower above the cities as a result of the symbiotic life that derives its energy from the past and projects it into the future. Every city is distinguished by its peculiar touch. Narrow winding streets crisscross with modern avenues and boulevards. New homes and condominiums are built in the shadow of Roman, medieval, or Renaissance palaces that are covered by the dark dust of time and the early fog of autumn and winter. If, at first sight, the air of the cities does not appear to be jovial, a ray of sunlight may suddenly lift the fog and reveal to the astonished visitor the inner sophistication and incomparable joy of lively places.

The Northern industrial triangle, which consists of Genoa, Turin, and Milan, is complemented by the amenities of Florence, Venice, and Bologna. In recent years, these cities have seen an influx of immigrants from the South to the North. Agriculture, manufacturing, and processing industries offer employment opportunities. The post-war economic boom transformed this area into an industrial giant that became the backbone of the Italian economy. Factually, Italy's government paid more attention to the North. The gap between the prosperous regions of the Center-North and the poor regions of the South widened.

The Center-South

"A diamond in the rough," indicates that quality and substance are encased in a mixture of unrefined materials, waiting for the work of skilled craftsmen who will bring out the sparkling gem. **Il Mezzogiorno** is the Italian area in the shape of a boot whose peripheral tip appears to caress Sicily, making the island an integral part of "foot" and "ankle." Endowed with natural beauty, this area offers breathtaking panoramas. The visitor can go back to the past by glancing at sights such as ancient theaters, temples, and cities that revisit the mysteries of antiquity. The areas of the *Mezzogiorno* with their amenities were the idyllic residences of mythological gods and goddesses and those in search of a better life. Man's desire to progress, explore, and build gave birth to places pulsating with life. Splendor, grace, glory, and creativity crowned Southern Italy. The sloping mountains descended into the sea to be washed by clean, foamy, blue waters. The fiery volcanoes enriched its soil in unparalleled ways, making agriculture a mainstay to this day. Sicily was called **il granaio d'Italia,** the granary of Italy. These lands are prosperous because of the mild climate and the rich soils. For centuries, agriculture has produced not only grains, but also lemons, oranges, olives, potatoes, sugar beets, tobacco, tomatoes, and livestock.

Nature has provided a meandering, jagged coastline that, for centuries, artists, scholars, and military geniuses found irresistible. Phoenicians, Greeks, Arabs, Romans, Normans, the French, Spaniards, and others lived or ruled over parts of the area, leaving their mark of culture on its soil.

Today this image is blurred by unemployment, political crises, terrorism, and organized crime. Agriculture is neglected. The **extra-comunitari** (legal and illegal immigrants from the neighboring countries) are the new hired hands who work in the fields.

Today the young generation prefers to find jobs in the local factories. There is an exodus from the poor rural villages toward the big cities of Italy and Europe. **Sole, pizza e amore** (sun, pizza, and love) are the cheerful notes strummed on the strings of a guitar by a Neapolitan street singer. The government has made an attempt to curb this movement by helping to build industrial plants such as Alfa Romeo, Fiat, Ital-Sider, Peugeot, paper mills, and atomic power stations. But these "cathedrals in the desert," as people call them, have not resolved any social problems. Too many politicians and their associates have found ways, in the public opinion, to line their pockets. A type of laissez-faire attitude has developed.

Corruption and "who you know" remain the principles on which things are done—and even a job (**il posto**) is obtained.

In spite of all the socio-economic issues, the *Mezzogiorno* of today is much more than spaghetti, mafia, and forgotten people! It is a fantastic, intriguing place that needs to be rediscovered. The years of political neglect have covered it with a film that hides the "diamond." Yet help may already be on the way. The internet of modern road arteries has brought even the most remote mountain villages out of isolation. Both national and international seaports and airports are well-equipped to allow the flow of products and passengers to and from all countries in the world. The emerging countries around the Mediterranean will enable the *Mezzogiorno* to become a commercial crossroads of the future. Modern villas and resort areas continue to stimulate and attract tourism with their combination of unspoiled natural beauty and a touch of fresh and innovative creations. Illiteracy has been almost eradicated. Education is the key to success and Southern Italy has the highest number of educated youths in the country with high school and college diplomas. Even though "intellectual unemployment" has been on the rise, the young people of the *Mezziogiorno* are the talented individuals whose preparation, energy, and creativity are needed for the revitalization of the region. They are the untapped energy that the Italian political leaders of today should use to build the infrastructures of an industrialized South. *Il Mezzogiorno* should be re-energized with an infusion of capital for the training of young people and the establishment of an industrial network that utilizes the "commercial potential" of the South while expanding and reinforcing the productive sectors of the North.

In the last decade, the United States alone has built about 100 industrial plants in the South. France, Germany, Switzerland, and England have put up more than 110 other plants. Foreign investors are present in almost every sector: mechanics, electronics, electric, chemical, plastics, food, manufacturing, metallurgy, and paper goods. To date, the car industry, led by the group FIAT, has built more than nineteen plants in the *Mezzogiorno*. The foreign investors have access to the Italian and European markets and can take advantage of the available work force. Thus, despite the problems of the past, the road to the future for the region looks more and more promising.

Continuing Controversy

The latest controversy on the subject of the differences between North and South has been generated by the publication of *L'Inferno, Profondo Sud, Male Oscuro* by Giorgio Bocca (Mondadori Editore, 1992). The diagnosis provided by the author is that **il Mezzogiorno è un inferno** (the *Mezzogiorno* is hell) and as a cure he suggests that **l'Italia deve dividersi in due** (Italy must split into two.) This is a hot issue where

North versus South, and has resulted in a face-to-face debate between Bocca, who is a journalist from Piedmont, and Giuseppe Galasso, a historian and college professor from Naples. Bocca maintains that there is a visible difference between North and South. While the North keeps producing in order to achieve wealth and prosperity, the South has abandoned agriculture and thinks that it can keep going forever on state salaries and pensions. Galasso, on the other hand, sustains that it is in the best interest of the country to keep the nation united. Southerners have greatly contributed to the prosperity of the North. The Alfa Romeo was founded by a Neapolitan and even the newspaper, *Corriere della Sera,* which is published in Milan, was established by another Neapolitan. He maintains that Italians need reforms and a national renewal.

Such tensions are not surprising. Despite its antiquities, Italy is a young nation. Most of the peninsula was not united as an independent country until 1861, and Rome became its capital only in 1871. The history of Italy has influenced Western civilization for centuries. The Roman Empire introduced law and order, language unity, arts, and architecture to many people. After the collapse of the Roman Empire in A.D. 476, Italy was divided into many small states and city-states governed by local and foreign rulers. For much of its history the popes controlled lands in central Italy, and the emperors from Germany had influence in the northern part of the peninsula. In the Middle Ages and also in the Renaissance—which began in Italy around the year 1300—cities such as Florence and Venice were able to be independent and gain control over much of the territory surrounding them. However, after the Renaissance Italy was dominated by foreign powers and was a pawn in larger international stakes. During this period, people's loyalty and identity tended to focus on the local, rather than on the idea of a nation. Only in the nineteenth century did nationalist movements gain strength in Italy, resulting in the ultimate unification of the peninsula under the king of Savoy. Later Italy became the war theater for European rulers competing for territory and political prestige. After World War II, Italy recaptured her place among the great nations of the world. When the North and South seriously strive to unify in common efforts to provide work and prosperity for all the people, there will be no limit to Italy's future rewards.

❁

65. *TU, LEI, AND VOI*

Tu, Lei, and **voi** (you) are all used in Italian to address other people.

Tu is used with friends, family, and pets.

Lei is used in formal address and when *tu* would not be used.

Dottoressa! Lei è molto gentile con i pazienti.	(Doctor! You are very polite with your patients.)

Voi is sometimes used to show respect toward an elderly person or someone in a higher social status. It is also used when addressing more than one person.

When in doubt, use *Lei*.

❁

66. *LA VENDEMMIA*

La vendemmia, the grape harvest, is a popular time in Italy. Grapes are usually hand-picked from the vines by itinerant workers or hired hands who travel from farm to farm to perform this valued service. Grapes are harvested around the seventh of September. After selection of the finest grapes, the workers take a break to eat some cheese, usually **caciocavallo** (cow's milk cheese in a round shape), with home-baked bread, as well as to drink local wine. The carefully picked grapes are transported to a central location and deposited into the **recipiente** (collection vat). It is a common practice for a collective to make the wine. When the grapes are pressed, the alcoholic and sugar levels are measured to determine the quality of the wine they will produce, and thus a price is fixed for the farmers who have sent them there. However, the farmers have already set aside enough grapes to make their own special ''nectar of the gods'' on their own property according to the old ways: hand-pressing with old-fashioned equipment.

By November eleventh, Saint Martin's Day, the grapes have been transformed into wine, which is sampled for the first time on that day. In Sicily, **pane di San Martino** (St. Martin's bread), which is a lightly sweetened hard biscuit with fennel seeds, is eaten as people eagerly sip the new wine. Some even use this time for a picnic to celebrate the new wine: **Salute!** (To your health!).

La vendemmia is a delightful, happy time of the year. The god of wine, Bacchus, is still alive and present in the mind of the **vendemmiatori** (harvesters). While work is in progress, folk songs fill the air of the **vigneto** (vineyard). The songs evoke the beauty of pastoral love and the simple life. Wine producers celebrate the event with festivities. The space in front of the farmhouse becomes **una pista da ballo** (a dance floor) for the young and young at heart and anyone wishing to relax and be merry. The dulcet tone of an accordion and the strum of a guitar and mandolin create a gay atmosphere. If you stop for a moment, you could hear Giuseppe Verdi's aria **Libiamo ne' calici che la bellezza infiora . . .!** (Let's drink from the mirth-giving cup that beauty adorns) from *La traviata*. It is a time for **brindisi** (toasts).

The **sagre** (feasts) have become part of the Italian way of life. In Marino, a town outside of Rome, the city fountain flows with wine to celebrate the grape harvest. There are many *sagre* celebrated in various ways throughout the country: **la sagra del granturco** (corn festival), **la sagra della polenta** (cornmeal festival), **la sagra del pesce** (fish festival).

67. VISITING

La visita manifests itself in a variety of ways. Family and friends enjoy getting together informally for **una partita alle carte** (a card game), **uno spuntino** (a quick bite), or simply just to drop in to say hello. Friendly visits may not last long; in fact, they usually take up less than a half-hour. Nothing is brought by the visitor, and neither does the visitor expect to be served any food or a cup of coffee.

Le visite di dovere (required visits) generally are made in times of mourning, bereavement, congratulations (marriage and religious occasions such as First Communions).

68. WAITING IN LINE

Fare la coda or **mettersi in coda** (to form a line) ought to be common in a nation of art, music, love, and civility—but it's not. Though semblances of queues can be found throughout Italy, it is not unusual for someone who is in a hurry (**una persona che non aspetta il suo turno**) to edge his or her way up to the front of the line despite the jeers and complaints of the patient waiters: **un gomito qua, un gomito là** (an elbow here, an elbow there).

Banks have begun to deal with people who enter and place their documents beneath all of the others. When bank patrons enter, they place their banking documents on the counter immediately in front of the teller. And the papers at the bottom are the first to be handled. So it is an advantage to have one's papers on the bottom. Recently, a Rome bank asked its patrons to obtain **uno scontrino** (a ticket) at a ticket dispenser inside the establishment, and above each teller numbers flash in consecutive order to signal who will be taken care of next. There is no chance for **il gomito** (the elbow). In fact, though some of the patrons may anxiously try to appeal to the tellers, the bank personnel make reference to the numerical system in place. Italy is becoming more progressive in this respect as it enters the twenty-first century.

69. WAYS OF CONVEYING INFORMATION

Italians delight in using colorful and poetic language. Italian is very musical and has a lyrical rhythm, which Italians tend to exploit. They are prone to put forth ideas in a meandering fashion as opposed to the directness of the Anglo-Saxon speaker. Many times Italians may side-track or take off on tangents and express themselves in convoluted and complex ways to elaborate on a topic. In order not to lose the listener, the speaker may use expressions such as **ritornando a quello che stavo dicendo** (going back to what I was saying before) or **come stavo dicendo prima** (as I was saying before). **Permettimi una parentesi** (allow me to interject) is used to further clarify a presentation with supporting statements. It is always a pleasant experience to listen and watch Italians interacting and gesturing upon matters of little or great importance, each with equal passion. (See article 26, ''Gestures.'')

70. WE MAKE LOVE, NOT WAR

Vivamus . . . atque amemus, (let us live . . . and let us love) echo the words of the great Roman poet Catullus who was born in Verona in A.D. 87. Italians live in a country kissed by the sun, loved by nature, and graced by the creative spirit of many geniuses. The environment is conducive to expressions of deep feelings. The spirit of Catullus has influenced the Italian way of life for centuries. The love theme has been a conditioning factor in literature, music, painting, sculpture, and cinematography since the beginning of the Italian language.

Love and Literature

As in many cultures, the theme of love is a predominating one. In Medieval Sicily, the minstrel Cielo d'Alcamo (1231), in one of his contrasts, depicts two lovers. The man asks for love, and the young lady plays hard to get. He declares his devotion, speaks of his power and wealth, and uses the most gallant expressions of love. She is reluctant and, while proclaiming to be untouchable, threatens to go back to her parents.

With Dante, Petrarch, and Boccaccio we see the three aspects of love. In Dante (1265-1321), the lady is an angel **che dà per li occhi una dolcezza al core** (who generates pleasure in the heart of her lover when she admires him). A man who is touched by love betters himself. In his ***Divina Commedia*** (The Divine Comedy) Paolo and Francesca, two of the most famous lovers in literature, are bound by their deep, illicit love for each other, and reminisce of "their kiss" that caused them death.

According to Petrarch (1304-1374), the first modern poet, love is a lament, a sensual attraction, and melancholy, though it can be cruel and beautiful. Boccaccio (1313-1375) reveals the love and passion of everyday people. His lovers in *Decameron* are more voluptuous, more hedonistic. Machiavelli (1469-1527), in *Mandragola,* illustrates the world of intrigues, deception, and persuasion that allows the young lover to win the graces and favors of a married young lady. The world of Boiardo (1441-1494), Ariosto (1474-1533), and Tasso (1544-1595) is filled with love stories and adventures of errant knights. They create dreamy love encounters where fantasy and reality blend. Angelo Poliziano (1454-1494) speaks about **le dolci acerbe**

109

cure che dà Amore (the tender loving pains inflicted by Love). "La Primavera" by Sandro Botticelli (Florence, 1445–1510) shows the world of "Graces." They are elegant, ethereal, and diaphanous. These idealized goddesses inspire men to love and appreciate beauty. The painting "Apollo and Daphne" by Pollaiolo (1426–1498) illustrates the tireless efforts of a pursuing lover and his disappointment when his love eludes him totally. "La Gioconda" by Leonardo da Vinci (1452–1519) is touching with her sweet, mysterious, and sardonic smile. Is she thinking about her spurned lover or is she enticing him with her uncommon beauty? Michelangelo Buonarroti (1475–1564) could be considered by many to be the founder of modernism. His sculptures of Bacco and David emphasize the harmony and elegance of the human body in a new way.

The theme of love is still treated in modern literature. The first Italian novel, *I promessi sposi* (1825–1827), is the story of lovers who are separated by fate against the background of the wars and troubles of seventeenth-century Lombardy. It was written by Alessandro Manzoni, who is credited with trying to establish a form of written Italian literature based on the Florentine dialect. The poet Gabriele D'Annunzio (1863–1938) enchants his readers with his vain, sensual approach to love.

The Latin Lover

The matinee idols of the cinema such as Amedeo Nazzari, Marcello Mastroianni, Vittorio Gassman, and Giancarlo Giannini reveal the gamut of behaviors of Italian lovers in action. The Italian lover is supposed to attract, enchant, and seduce. He is overt in expressing his appreciation of the passing female. But does la dolce vita (the sweet life) really exist? How much is reality and how much is fantasy?

Who is this modern Italian latin lover? Is he a gigolo or a contemporary Don Juan with a particular physical aspect and a special appearance? He can be a young man who has charm and poise and knows how to treat a lady. He is everywhere: at outdoor cafes, parks, beaches, dancing clubs, airports, bus stops, or even just crossing the street. Women can be attracted to his inspiring sense of trust and his polite manners. He can provide a romantic walk under the starry Italian skies, surprise a woman with a serenade at a local restaurant, or even fascinate her with a gondola ride or a nocturnal view of the city panorama. The Italian Latin lover views himself as an irresistible stallion capable of making a woman feel loved and desired.

The Latin lover, however, is more myth than reality. The Italian man has been inhibited by religious and sexual taboos and today is thus frustrated by sex. There is more emphasis on what is said than done. The Italian male tries to be the **conquistatore** (a lady-killer) simply because he was raised in a climate of bragging inhibition. He feels scorned when he is betrayed by a loved one. Denigration by calling him **cornuto** (cuckold) is proven to be offensive and demeaning, and may lead to revenge or even murder to clear his reputation. There are unspoken matters that need no clarification or explanation; matters that are better left unsaid. The Latin lover goes through life in spasmodic episodes of playing Prince Charming, getting his princess, and living happily ever after until the next opportunity appears!

71. THE WINES OF ITALY

The fruit of the vine has its roots implanted deep in the history of Italy as far back as the Etruscan and Roman times. The soils varying from region to region, including the assistance of Mother Nature in mixing volcanic ash with the soil, enhance the bouquet and the flavor of Italian wines.

Wine is the Italian national drink and is served before, during, and after meals. It may be red, rosé, or white, and it may be chilled, warm, delicate, sweet, robust, or sparkling. Italians may drink wine with salads and may intermix varieties because they view drinking wine as natural and healthful. **Un bel bicchiere di vino** (a good glass of wine), served from large flasks or pitchers, cements friendships and welcomes guests into the house. **Il vino fatto in casa** (homemade wine) is still enjoyed and appreciated for its natural qualities, color, bouquet, and taste.

Italian wines are as diverse as the mosaic of the Italian culture. From the north to the south, wines change just as the geography and customs change from region to region.

72. WOMEN

The image of the modern Italian woman is dynamic, attractive, and educated. She has emerged in contemporary society as effective in professional life, as the successful politician, doctor, lawyer, entrepreneur, and industrial leader. However, she has also kept her role at the heart of the home. The image of the affectionate, family-oriented homemaker continues alongside the more contemporary role. The Italian woman has liberated herself from her former subjugation to her husband. Now she, too, is a bread-winner. She is self-sufficient, independent, competitive, and a driving force in society.

In 1974, Italians voted for the right of divorce in a referendum. This newly added freedom has seen many women become heads of households and contributed to the zero growth of population. Prearranged marriages have disappeared. The Italian woman has freedom of movement and choice. Only a few years ago, life in villages and small towns had women live under close scrutiny by family members. Her acquaintances and her dates were selected and chaperoned. The family name and reputation were at stake. Today many young women go to school and work in cities away from the family. They get behind the wheel of their cars and experience independence and responsibility for making their own choices.

And what then has become the role of the Italian male? Does he have to share in the domestic responsibilities of cleaning the house and of child rearing? Who does the cooking? These questions can be answered in the modern vernacular: this is the twenty-first century, the Age of the Woman! The new age has placed new meaning on the word *sharing.* In the past, the idea was "This is your job and this is my job." Now the attitude is, "If you have the time and the opportunity, you do it." This further translates, "If you are home before me, you start dinner. If I have to bring work home, you wash the clothes or vacuum the rugs." The Western male's role has changed into one of sharing responsibilities for the running of the home, and raising the children.

73. WORK

Italians have always been work-oriented. The father has traditionally been considered the provider. The mother took care of the house and the children. As times changed and Italy became one of the industrialized nations of the world, both husband and wife found themselves in new roles as workers, sometimes working side by side in industry and at home. Education has played a pivotal role in preparing women for the workplace by giving them skills and training. Italian women occupy a prominent place in modern society, acquiring leadership positions in the business and academic worlds.

The new generation of Italians has tended to move away from manual jobs, which are performed more and more with the help of immigrants to Italy. Trades such as tailoring, embroidery, jewelry making, and careers in mechanical fields still require specific training. Italians are highly dedicated workers and are typically treated with fairness and dignity by their superiors and employers. Workers have a vested interest in their companies, and they receive monetary benefits, even if the factory closes, in proportion to the number of years of service to the company. However, Italians do not live to work but work to enjoy life. The median retirement age is about fifty. One can expect to be granted a **buona uscita** (a bonus) on retirement. This signifies the end of a successful and productive work experience.

74. THE WORLD OF YOUTH

Youth and Their Music

What kind of music appeals to the young Italians of today? Do opera, folk music, and Neapolitan tunes still appeal to the young? Older Italians may remember with nostalgia **la musica melodica** (melodic music) of such singers as Giorgio Consolini, Nilla Pizzi, and Claudio Villa. Somewhat younger ones may remember **gli urlatori** (pop singers) such as Tony Dallara and Adriano Celentano. However, like young people all the over the world, Italian youth are in tune with the latest trends in music and popular international styles and singers.

Rap

Although rap has been popular in the United States for quite some time, Italy's young people have only recently begun to listen to it. They say **C'è rap e rap** (which means "There's rap and there's rap). They differentiate between **violento, incazzato, ammazza-poliziotti** (violent, fanatic, police-killer) rap and softer, more musical rap. There is also political rap (**il rap iperpoliticizzato**).

It seems that the rappers (**i parolai**) occupy a stable position on the scene of Italian music because many Italian young people prefer "words" to harmony. **Luca Carboni**, the **99 Posse**, l'**Orchestra Italiana**, and the hip-hop storyteller **Frankie Hi-Nrg Mc** uses strong words amplified by the rhythm, or faint words sustained by melody.

Also recently, disk jockeys mix music to the speeches of prominent political figures. And famous literary compositions have become part of **la poesia-rap** (rap poetry), including such works as *San Martino* by Giosuè Carducci, *L'Infinito* by Giacomo Leopardi, and *Il cinque maggio* by Alessandro Manzoni. In this way, classic literature may become part of the everyday life of youth.

Rock Music

Rock music has been popular in Italy since the days of the Beatles and the Rolling Stones. Groups such as Nirvana, Pearl Jam, and the Lemonheads are popular in Italy. But who are the most famous Italian rock stars (**rochettari**) of the 1990s?

883, which is the name used by Max Pezzali and Mauro Ripetti of Pavia, direct their music to young people who like simple, catchy tunes. The values and interests of the duo reflect those of many of their contemporaries: family life, attending school, reading comics, listening to all types of music.

Other singers take a more politically engaged approach, discussing sex, abortion, AIDS, drugs, and other political issues. Piero Pelù, of the Litfiba groups, sings about sexual freedom and the legalization of drugs. He extorts his fans not to believe in the "remade" politicians (**i politici rinnovati**). Francesco De Gregori is an example of singer/songwriter (**cantautore**). He sings about current issues, expressing himself in poetic metaphors. Renato Zero maintains that society is not livable (**la società è invivibile**) and that the young generation must build one that offers music, brotherhood, and pure love. He is against drugs and abortion, and he believes in praying—and the existence of fairy godmothers! Antonello Venditti sings about love and says in Roman dialect **volemose bene noatri** (let's love each other). Eros Ramazzotti sings about family values, while Lucio Dalla finds inspiration in traditional Neapolitan music and religion.

More recently, there is grunge, born as a musical movement in American basements. This "underground" form of music reached Italy in the early 1990s. Grunge is **neo-pauperista e post-ecologista** (new poverty and post ecology). It is characterized by deep, rough sounds, and considers music the most important means of communication.

Youth and Fashion

A high school (**liceo**) is probably the best place to go to observe the fashions of young people. You probably will see a mix of styles in clothing and fashion. Some young people may be dressed in black, while another group wears Mexican ponchos and others have adopted **lo stile leonca-vallino** with boots and long leather coats. Many may sport jeans, sneakers, and sweaters, while others follow the loose elegant Armani style. Then there are those who follow the **neopovero** ("new" poor) style, wearing oversized clothes in gaudy colors that seem to be thrown together. This latter group represent the Italian grunge. In Italy, this style from the United States can be characterized as **sporco, stropicciato** (dirty and creased). One sign of a follower of the grunge is the classic baseball cap, worn backwards. Followers of the grunge style may also wear extra large plaid shirts, black leather jackets, and wornout jeans. Their socks, visible above their military boots, may not match.

Youth and Their Love Life

Older people may accuse the youth of today of being arrogant and without manners, while others may see them as sincere and shy with a strong desire for freedom and self-determination. Italian teenagers seem to be abandoning the old slogan of **Facciamo l'amore non la**

guerra (Let's make love, not war) to return **all'antico** (to the old ways). Teenagers are searching for romantic love and a simple life. The A.I.E.D. (**Associazione italiana per l'educazione demografica**) indicates that the children of the generation that preached free love are shy and bashful sweethearts. They are not in a rush to experience premature sex. Couples tend to be loyal to each other and stay together longer. This attitude has changed their behavior in school. There is less off-color graffiti, and displays of affection in hallways may be limited to an occasional kiss. (For more information, see article 17, "Dating and marriage.")

❁

SOURCES AND RELATED READINGS

Barzini, Luigi. *The Italians*. Macmillan, 1977.

Bethemont, Jacques, and Pelletier, Jean. *Italy: A Geographical Introduction*. Longman, 1983.

Battaglino, Lina, editor, *La Barzelletta: Carabinieri, Sexi, Automobilisti*. Editrice "La Lucciola," Varese, Italy, 1991.

Epoca-Settimanale N. 2187-9-09-1992. A. Mondadori Editore, Casella postale N. 1833, Milano, pages 48-50.

Grizzuti Harrison, Barbara. *Italian Days*. Weidenfeld & Nicolson, 1989.

Hoffman, Paul. *Cento Città: A Guide to the "Hundred" Cities and Towns of Italy*. Henry Holt and Company, 1988.

Kogan, Norman. *A Political History of Italy: The Postwar Years*. Praeger, 1983.

LaPalombara, Joseph. *Democracy, Italian Style*. Yale University Press, 1989.

Norwich, John Julius, editor. *The Italians: History, Art, and the Genius of a People*. Abrams, 1983.

Procacci, Giuliano. *History of the Italian People*. Harper, 1970.

Simon, Kate. *Italy: The Places In Between*. Harper & Row, 1984.

Spalding, Henry, ed. *Joys of Italian Humor and Folklore*. Jonathan David, 1980.

INDEX

INDEX